Hypnotic Control

Reflections on the Nature of Staged Influence

John-Ivan Palmer

WHISTLING SHADE
PRESS

Saint Paul, MN
www.whistlingshade.com

First Edition, First Printing

April 2025

ISBN 978-0-9829335-1-0

Book and cover design by Joel Van Valin

Printed in the United States of America

Also by John-Ivan Palmer:

Motels of Burning Madness

Master of Deception

For Harue

Contents

Preliminary Note   9

1 - Trance   13

1 - Stage Hypnotism and the Annihilation of Rational Thought   14

II - Self   29

2 - Lounge Act Poet Blown Away   30

3 - Sway Back   51

4 - Murder in a Chicken Suit: The Semanticist and Lana Turner's Last Husband   61

5 - Can You Hear Me Back There? Influence and the Amplified Voice   77

III - Culture   93

6 - Death by Projected Thought   94

7 - Twins Joined at the Forehead: Hypnosis and TV   103

8 - Those People: Hate and the Hypnotic Other   116

9 - Mesmer Made Me Do It: Mass Murder in Schools   126

10 - You Call Me Violent I Kill You: Terror and Trance   139

11 - The Anointed One Will Be with You Shortly   144

12 - Trump and the Q Trick   152

13 - Listen Only to My Voice: Cults   159

14 - A Note on Proof   163

Conclusion   166

Bibliography and Name Index   170

Preliminary Note

On or about February 1778, human character changed. Someone named Anton stumbled upon an artifact of consciousness that had long remained hidden in the sands of the obvious. He was not the first to transmit invisible waves of influence, but he was the first to put it in a box and give it a name—"animal magnetism"—also referred to by his last name as "mesmerism," later changed to "hypnotism." In that axial year he found he could apply a specific formula of influence to manipulate people into acts of unbelievable absurdity. He convinced them to touch a container of this "animal magnetism," which was actually nothing more than suggested stuff. It made them hit the floor twitching. They laughed, they cried, they kissed their brains good-by. The behavior was so extreme and spread so rapidly that King Louis XVI appointed a Royal Commission to investigate.[1]

Hypnotism is a fashion, and fashion changes.[2] What we see as trance today is not the trance of ten, fifty, a hundred, two hundred years ago. When it began in Paris, people responded by collapsing to the floor. A few decades later a mesmerist could attract a huge crowd by burying a hypnotized subject alive for days, then digging him up alive and bowing to applause. When that went out of vogue, it was piercing subjects with hat pins and sewing them together with carpet thread. More applause. Then it was displaying them in a department

---

1 An English translation of the Commission's 1784 report can be found at the National Archives (US) website: founders.archives.gov/documents/Franklin/01-42-02-0304

2 See two articles by Jonathan Miller, "Magnetic Mockeries" in *Social Research*, vol. 68, Fall, 2001, pp. 717-739; and "Going Unconscious" in *Hidden Histories of Science*, ed. Robert B. Silvers (1995), pp. 1-35.

store window, slumped in a chair all day for the amusement of passers-by. Today it's the disguised zap-out of strangers before a hidden camera and—surprise!—the X-rated performance.

Whether one does or does not accept the existence of the hypnotic state (conclusions have never been unanimous), there is no disputing that people respond to suggestion, sway, domination, and control. Hypnotists who exhibit human beings in a state of heightened suggestibility traditionally begin with the false assurance that no one will "do anything they wouldn't ordinarily do," and then, in complete contradiction, make people think they're quacking ducks, talk with their mouth stuck open, catch a fish in their pants, or buzz around the audience like a human fly.

It's called hypnotic control.

Such a thing is not appropriate for most occasions, but where it is (comedy clubs, casinos, high school post-proms) the spectacle of people manipulated beyond what defines them as human generates a peculiar kind of laughter, an over-the-top, ultra-mega turbocharged hysteria that most people have never experienced. It's dismissed with the stigmatizing phrase "mere entertainment." Some consider it dangerous.

In 1940 the Hungarian philosopher Helmuth Plessner[1], known for his analysis of historical absurdities such as the Third Reich, wrote that laughter, if it occurs at the expense of someone else, becomes the "basest mode of sociability." The hypnotic exhibition is an event of abject baseness where human beings are manipulated by suggestion into positions of extreme social disadvantage. A hypnotic subject trying to walk in what they think are fifty-pound shoes in front of a laughing crowd exactly fits Plessner's description. After years of exerting hypnotic control of others, I woke up to the realization that this mode of influence was exerting itself back on me. Control is addictive, especially absolute control, and when I began to see myself as hooked on turning people into monkeys and washing machines for personal reward, my ego began to stand out too much.

---

1 *Lachen und Weinen. Eine Untersuchung nach den Grenzen menschlichen Verhaltens* (1941) translated as *Laughing and Crying, a Study of the Limits of Human Behavior* (1970).

Hypnotizing people for entertainment is nothing I would "ordinarily do" either. The practice held no particular fascination for me and was never a hobby. As often happens in any line of work, it's something I backed into—perhaps why I can look at the practice more objectively than someone who evangelizes either for or against it. It was never my goal in life. A source of income, yes. A will to power, definitely. I've been doing it a very long time, but I would rather have been a poet.

As the only son of a traveling floor show magician[1], I had little aptitude for employment, and my attempts in those areas were dismal (proofreader, shoe-shiner, butterfly farmer). I had no control over my destiny. When my father saw me drifting toward the life of a poetry-writing derelict, he urged me to learn a few simple magic tricks and blend in the practice of hypnotism. With his usual pontifical fatherliness he said, "That's where the money is." He held great prestige in my mind, so I followed his suggestion even though show business never interested me. I didn't know at first what I was getting into. Maybe I never knew until I was no longer in it.

With drugged hippies as my first subjects, it grew into a shoddy show in schools and strip clubs and eventually a career. A plumber sees the world as pipe. A hairdresser sees the world as hair. To me the world is a place where people think there's a flower growing out of their head. I see influence and control everywhere and wonder why everyone else doesn't see it too. It could be they haven't experienced the baptisms of fire I had to go through to arrive at such a realization.

I don't have to be told that my window onto the world faces a back alley. But the window is there nonetheless, and through it I see everyone's actions, beliefs and conclusions, their absolute certainties and smallest mundanities as the result of persuasive influence. These workings are, of necessity, hidden in plain view, otherwise they would be self-neutralizing. A person would never pray to an idol, bray like a donkey, or murder classmates on Hitler's birthday, unless they fully believed it's what they should do. Since influence in the extreme has been my occupation, if not my preoccupation, all of it strikes me as quite natural and expected.

---

1 See *Master of Deception* (2020).

If deviation from the world of normalcy into the world of lunacy (and back again) were not possible—or in my case so outlandishly funny and profitable—I would not have had a livelihood. But eventually my sense of omnipotence was replaced by the sense I was committing an outrage, albeit a largely entertaining one. The writer in me that had long been subsumed to the mesmeric practice re-emerged, and the "subject" of the writing became the very practice that subsumed it. What follows is the result.

I - Trance

1 - Stage Hypnotism and the Annihilation of Rational Thought

People overestimate the persistence of so-called "sanity." In only minutes, a theatrical hypnotist like myself can spoon out a person's rational mind like the yolk from a hard-boiled egg. It's a lot easier than a therapist trying to put Humpty Dumpty back together again. Through suggestion alone, hypnotized subjects, otherwise sane and cogent citizens, some quite intelligent, others not so much, become wash machines, crying babies, braying donkeys, or statues fixed in frozen poses picked up and moved about the stage (*"Here come the pigeons!"*). They jump, they shake, they shout their lungs out and flail at imaginary pests. They are "awakened" and sent back to the audience with posthypnotic suggestions where, upon the signal of a hand gesture or a certain word, they jump to their feet and act out a given command, such as yelling "I lost my butt!" (*"What does it look like, maybe we can help you find it?"*) When it's all over, the hypnotists say to their volunteers, *"You will feel better than ever before in your life!"*

Under his influence in the 1770s, Anton Mesmer's subjects hit the floor and snorted and screamed and tore at their clothes in his theater draped with purple curtains. He called this bizarre response *le crisis* (the seizure). The same behavior had been known throughout history in various forms of mass delusion, but Mesmer was the first to isolate it, give it a name, and make it start and stop on demand. Imitators sprang up soon enough and continued Mesmer's performances in the generations that followed down to myself and others. Although the word "hypnotism" is almost universally recognized, it remains a relatively unseen phenomenon as a staged performance. For those who have witnessed—or experienced—a hypnotism show, it exists as a memory, conveyed by word of mouth, and therefore a myth.

After my exhibitions, the stage is littered with the debris of this myth—shoes, pens, wallets, earrings. Plenty of cell phones, pipes, lighters, vape caps and pens fallen from pockets. Occasionally a knife. I find clumps of hair caught in the joints of folding chairs, sometimes with a chunk of scalp attached. The cause of this devastation makes those who see it laugh to a point of such intense apoplexy as to be literally painful. An essential element is its immediacy—in other words, you have to be there. To the subjects it's unassailable reality. To clinicians concerned with mental health it's the sort of thing they want to see outlawed. To me it's a living.

Stage hypnotism is not a fine art. It's to the stage what the Styrofoam cup is to stemware. Compared to opera, theater, symphony, it's down-market amusement that defies preservation. What's to preserve? There's no script or score as with a play or concert. Even if you visually record someone who thinks he's a human jackhammer, shaking so violently his glasses fly off, it loses much of its impact on replay. You don't see any more the second time around and you laugh somewhat less. It's like telling the same joke twice.

There are others, however, who regard this spectacle as a portal to other realms of consciousness, as was the case in the nineteenth century, with the widespread popularity of self-hypnotized spirit mediums. To Schopenhauer hypnotism was the "most significant discovery ever made." New Age catalogues have sections on hypnosis that promise to help you find your spirit guide, project you into the apocalypse, help you remember your flight on a UFO. And then there are those who think it's fake (while at the same time succumbing to other suggestions). Psychologists in the behaviorist school regard hypnotism as nothing more than a conditioned response, no different than B. F. Skinner teaching pigeons to play Ping Pong.[1] But as long as the naysayers stay in the minority, the believers

---

1 Original black and white footage at youtube.com/watch?v=vGazyH6fQQ Short sections are awkwardly spliced together to make the staged "game" seem longer than it really is. Skinner used the term "superstition" to describe non-compliance to stimulus. See *Journal of Experimental Psychology* (1948), Vol. 38, pp. 168-172.

will drown them out, which has always been the case. All that matters is that it looks convincing enough for the audience to lose sufficient presence of mind and fall into table-pounding, eye-watering, throat choking, sphincter-bursting hysterics.

My childhood as a show business kid did not prepare me for the mainstream, (or life as a poet, for that matter), but it did provide certain opportunities for an alternative source of income. Before I fell into dereliction or a life of crime, I began a career in the most predatory, downright vampiric of all occupations. The demand was not widespread, but where it existed, I could wheel out a routine that at its best worked well enough to keep me solvent. Ultimately, as long as the audience got what it wanted, I stayed in business.

I heard stage hypnotism once described as the most powerful social influence phenomenon known to man. The key word is "social." It's a matrix of interactions between self, subjects and audience. I'm commonly asked what kind of person is easy to hypnotize, and the answer to that question is crucial to making it work. Occupations that deal with *people*—social workers, medical professionals, teachers, cops—yield a higher percentage of promising subjects. But watch out for engineers, architects, computer programmers, mechanics and bankers. They are in the *thing* business, and to them people (including themselves) are items that interact in a linear and mechanical way that has nothing to do with the artifice of trance (my version of stage trance, at least). Youth is the hypnotic Garden of Eden and reproductive optimizers are more open to the experience of losing their mind in public. Hypnotists thrive on high school pep rallies, assembly programs, proms. Colleges, biker dives and comedy clubs are always rife with hypnotic potential. A mesmeric desert on the other hand is an audience where out across the tops of heads I see nothing but pink and gray, the colors of entrenched thought, the hardest to depotentiate. If the hypnotist is skilled enough, he or she can have it in for them too, maybe not to the point of putting their pants on backwards, but at least wearing their shoes on the wrong feet.

Curiously, an unpropitious audience is one made up of artists and avant-gardists. Or, God forbid, poets. They already annihilate rational thought by virtue of what they do. How can you annihilate what is already annihilated? To deconstruct accepted behavior, there has to be a consensus on that behavior to begin with. Artists have made that deconstruction long before they walk through the door. There's nothing left to deconstruct. Moreover, they tend not to be in the people business the same way as nurses and cops. (An exception is actors, who make excellent subjects.) Most of the hypnotic subjects in André Breton's surrealist séances were not really in a state of "hypnosis," but only "found themselves forced to simulate to keep the 'mouth of shadows' speaking."[1] Fortunately, he did not have to depend on it for a living.

The behavior of a subject is never completely predictable and surprises both good and bad are always possible. My strategy is to take probabilistic advantage of certain people (very roughly one in ten) who are capable of whatever it is that results in the appearance of being in a trance. A sword of Democles—failure—always hangs over me. I could find myself facing an audience with a stage full of duds who aren't responding. To a hypnotist this is death. It's a humiliation *worse* than death. It's why hypnotists, more than most performers, are hyper-focused at showtime because—as with wire walkers—the risks and consequences are so extreme. If a musician hits a few wrong notes at least the song is played. If a comic doesn't get a laugh at least the joke is told. For a hypnotist the Fat Lady has to sing. If not... Prior to showtime everything is in a state of potential toward success as well as failure. Afterward, for better or for worse, it's actual, fixed, and beyond change.

Hypnotic probabilities are elusive, like veins of precious ore. I never know where they are going to be or where they are going to run. I am exquisitely sensitive to their signs, such as the geographic dimension. For some unknown reason, I can expect towns on hills or bodies of water to yield more somnambules than those on flat terrain. There are hypnotic hot

---

1 Georges Limbour, after having barked like a dog and eaten from the animal's dish while under hypnosis, later confessed to painter André Masson that the whole thing has been a setup, just to see Breton's reaction..." For other instances of subjects faking hypnosis for Breton, see Mark Polizotti, *Revolution of the Mind, the Life of André Breton* (1995), p181-183.

spots like Boise, Idaho, as well as hypnotic dead zones like Oostburg, Wisconsin. It's predictably consistent over time. If I go back to the same place ten years later, I get the same percentage, which is why I refer back to the detailed notes I take on every performance, like a gambler who calculates the wager based on which cards have been played. The closer to the equator, the better the subjects. I don't know why that should be. It's not the sort of thing that turns up in the psychological literature because it serves no purpose there—but it does to me. Perhaps changes of season necessitate future planning, which requires deductive reasoning (anti-trance), whereas tropical places have one season, an eternal now, and no need to think ahead (trance itself). Or it could be one of those anomalous phenomena, as Wilbur once wrote, that should not leave a fissure in the world if left unexplained.

I've also noticed that susceptibility runs in families. If a wife meows like a cat, so will the husband. And the kids. And grandma. And gramps. With religious groups the percentages are in my favor while New Agers are a hard push (see avant-gardists above). The geography of the body forms another demographic. Tattoos and scars indicate hypnotic proclivity. As to why, I'll guess that pain and body modification require a certain amount of dissociation congruent with trance. I've learned to watch out for people in black, because black symbolizes contraction of the social lens, and stage hypnotism is a social phenomenon. Working with them is not worth the chance of failure, but sometimes that's the hand I'm dealt and I have no choice but to play it. Outlaw bikers ride in packs because they're social, therefore biker bars are a pushover. When Big Moe, covered with tatts, steps up on stage, his pals assume I'm a goner. They'll give me a few brief moments to see how I'm going to crumble, but when Moe drops off his chair in a hypnotic trance, I become, as the Emperor Vespasian supposedly said, "like a god." The laugh dam bursts and for the rest of the night I won't have to buy my own drinks.

There are some people so easy to hypnotize that there arises another problem—failure to awaken. This is called "hypnotic abreaction," a phenomenon that has been the basis of efforts to ban public exhibitions almost from the moment they were created by Mesmer in the 1770s. Dr. Morris Kleinhauz, writing in the *International Journal of Clinical and Experimental Hypnosis* (1979, no. 3), challenges the actual legality of stage hypnotism in light of the many "untreated cases [of] psychiatric disturbances" he says it can cause. Its early signs, usually among females, are shaking, paralysis, hyperventilation, general distress and lack of response to the suggestion of waking up. It can quickly develop into crying, screaming and terrifying hallucinations, the classic symptoms of what used to be termed "hysteria." The much less common male abreaction may also involve hyperventilation, but if paralysis occurs it's usually in the lips so the subject can barely talk, sometimes to the point of total inability to speak (aphasia).

When these negative reactions occur, laughter stops. The show is no longer a hoot. The audience watches in dead silence as the hypnotist desperately tries to repair the damage. It's almost as bad as not being able to hypnotize anyone at all, but not quite, because at least with abreaction there's no doubt something has actually happened. There may be blame, but there's no humiliation from failure to perform. There have been cases where an abreacting subject has had to be carried from the premises screaming and taken by ambulance to a hospital and injected with anti-psychotic drugs. Dr. Frank MacHovec cites in *Hypnosis Complications* (1986) the case of a young woman in a hypnosis show, who became stuporous, unable to speak, swallowed her tongue and gasped for air as her eyes rolled up into their sockets. According to MacHovec, she had to be fed intravenously for months to stay alive.

An experienced hypnotist can spot and forestall these decompressions in their early stages, but those self-deluded phonies with their downloaded scripts can blow it big time. There have been tragic sequelae as in the case of Lynn Howarth in Britain who took six months to recover from a non-existent 10,000-volt shock through her chair.[1] Margaret Harper started the Campaign Against Stage Hypnotism in the UK after her

---

1 *London Times*, Dec. 14, 1994, p 16.

daughter died following participation in an especially rough hypnosis show.[1]

The sooner signs are spotted, the easier they are to correct. The subject should be gently awakened, dismissed back to the audience, and then carefully observed from the stage as the show proceeds. If she (or he) interacts with friends, that's a sign of normal re-integration. If she stares at the fronts and backs of her hands, wrestling with uncertain reality while the rest of the audience is laughing their heads off, there's a chance she may come backstage afterward complaining of "feeling funny," or saying she's "not completely out of it." At that point she needs to be re-hypnotized and given suggestions of relaxation combined with old-fashioned mesmeric stroking of the shoulder and arms, then slowly awakened, a technique that has always worked in my situations.

Abreaction does not occur often enough to be a constant problem, but enough to require constant vigilance. A headache here, a funny feeling there. Heavy feet, strange thoughts. *My ears are burning, I feel like I don't have a belly button. Why does it bother me that my fingers aren't all the same length? Did I really take off all my clothes? Why does my mouth taste like ice cream? I smell something no one else does. Why am I shaking?*

At an evening performance at the Casino Ballroom in Watertown, South Dakota, I was hanging up my tux in the dressing room when I heard something that sounded like the howling of a dog. As the sound grew closer, I realized it was a wailing woman. There was a knock on the door and when I opened it, I saw a small group of people carrying a young female subject from my demonstration. She was in distress because she could not walk. Her panic spread to the group that brought her, which in turn caused her more panic. This was a feedback situation common with victim and onlookers in abreaction cases. My first step was to separate her from her panicked friends, then close the door. I re-hypnotized her and told her that when she opened her eyes, she would have the poise of a ballet dancer, holding her head high as if wearing long earrings that hung down and touched her shoulders. After

---

1 *London Times*, Dec. 14, 1994, p. 8. The coroner officially ruled that Sharon Tabarn died from "natural causes," namely pulmonary edema.

waking her up she opened the door and walked out with the poise of a ballerina and joined her friends to their complete astonishment. I continued putting away my things.

In his short story "The Quantity Theory of Insanity," Will Self proposes through a fictional psychiatrist a fixed proportion of sanity available on the "surface of the collective psyche." The amount never varies, just shifts from one place to the next like pressing a spot on an old mattress, resulting in another part springing up. Similarly, if I remove an abreaction after a performance in South Dakota, it will only show up again somewhere else. So I'm constantly vigilant.

I have a strict rule that if one of my subjects has an abreaction I will work with that person for as long as it takes to bring them back to baseline consciousness. Almost never has it gone beyond fifteen minutes, but one time I did have to work by phone with a female subject, a nurse in Decatur, Iowa, who felt "not quite right" after my performance for a hospital group. I rehypnotized her repeatedly for two days by telephone until she was back to normal.

Going too far with influence is what stage hypnotism has always been about. In 1896 the mono-named Santanelli carried the human plank stunt further by stretching *two* subjects between saw horses, had *four* people stand on them, then stood on top of all *six* like the king of the mountain. That was only a warm-up. He commanded subjects to eat soap suds, thinking it was ice cream. And if even that was not enough, he made them drink a cocktail of cayenne pepper, vinegar, and oil, then had them rave over how delicious it was. But wait, there was even more. With a needle and long piece of carpet thread he sewed three hypnotized people together through the ears and lips. The audience went wild, and a front page feature the *New York Times* reported his "wonderful feats." Another marvel was to send a subject into the audience with his jaw locked open and invite anyone to try and close it. At Hammersein's Olympia theater one spectator decided to spit a wad of chewing tobacco down the subject's throat. The police were called and there were charges of assault. [1]

---

1 *New York Times*, April 20, 1896, p. 3.

At the Opera House in Woonsocket, Rhode Island, the incredible Professor Frank Farnsworth performed the human plank, but instead of having one or two or four people stand on the subject, he winched down a six-hundred-pound slab of stone. Just as a blacksmith started pounding it with a sledgehammer, the chairs gave way, and the subject was crushed to death,[1] along with, no doubt, the Professor's monstrous ego.

What passed for amusement then, would not pass the Geneva conventions today. Perhaps reflecting the conditions of life in the nineteenth century, it should not be surprising that hypnotic stunts involved pain, and plenty of it. Dentists were few and far between, and medical care was less available than whiskey and laudanum. Hypnotized subjects imbibed powerful emetics and laxatives before needles were inserted under the fingernails, flares lit on the surface of the skin, and tongues nailed to benches.

A hypnotized woman at the Folies Bergères was thrown like raw meat into a cage of lions. She was knocked around, but not eaten.[2] The applause no doubt was thunderous, but so was the outcry over what was called "a new kind of stimulus to jaded nerves."

Although this kind of publicity helped ticket sales at hypnosis shows, it also had an inhibiting effect when it came to getting volunteers. Not everyone wanted to buy a ticket for amusement only to be sewn to someone else like a button. Hypnotists solved this problem by using fake subjects known as "horses." Instead of trying to burn and impale volunteers from the audience, they simply paid a horse to grit their teeth and take it. Considering the times, being a horse wasn't much different than many other hard jobs, such as mining, farming, or serving in a regiment. The main difference was that hypno-horses officially did not exist. But here too, there were unintended consequences. The incredible Dr. Townsend made quite a sensation by using as many as six fake subjects to undergo all manner of torture for public amusement.[3] But when he decided not to pay one, the horse went public,

1 *New York Daily Tribune,* May 17, 1901.
2 *New York Times,* May 30, 1887.
3 *New York Times,* Feb. 26, 1885.

claiming his pain-enduring skill was simply a matter of "cultivation." After that *all* hypnotists were suspected of using horses, which had a negative effect on ticket sales.

When Edwin Boone advertised that he would bury a hypnotized subject alive in a Kentucky baseball field, two thousand people came to watch, probably more than would have turned out if the man had actually died. After two days, the anonymous subject was exhumed, face purple, sweating profusely, and heart rate at half that of a live person. The semi-corpse was taken by trolley to the local opera house and worked into the show, presumably to another large crowd. The emboldened Mr. Boone intended to take his burial act—and subject—to Cincinnati for a *seven*-day burial, and if he survived that, he was going to plant him in New York for *ten* days.[1] Audience response to someone buried in a hole that long will never be known because his subject snitched to the press that he was not hypnotized and Boone brought him food and water through a secret passageway. Instead of basking in glory, Boone basked in shame. Perhaps to the great relief of his horse.

Psychiatric literature universally refers to stage hypnotism with phrases like, "legislative control to eliminate," "legislation urgently required," "made illegal," "should be controlled by law," "eliminate the use of," and so forth. Dr. Harold B. Crasilneck, Ph. D. and Dr. James A. Hall, M.D., authors of *Clinical Hypnosis*, write that hypnosis "should be used only by licensed professionals." Dr. William Kroger's asserts in *Clinical and Experimental Hypnosis* that it "should be restricted to those qualified...for...treating medical and psychological disorders,"[2] and Dr. Frank MacHovec has stated in no uncertain terms that it should be practiced only by "postgraduate doctoral-level hypnosis diplomates in medicine [and] psychology." [3]

The British hypnotist and media star, Paul McKenna, is a perfect example of what Dr. MacHovec and others are against. At one of his performances, he gave Christopher Gates the suggestion that he had lost his penis. But Gates ended up losing

---

1 *New York Times,* Sep. 19, 1896.
2 p. 106.
3 *American Journal of Clinical Hypnosis,* Vol. 31, No. 1, July 1988, p. 40.

more than that, namely, his sanity. After McKenna got his laughs at Gates's expense, Gates claimed he heard the voices of Jesus and Moses, and developed a fear of showers and upstairs rooms. Strangely, there were no reports, in the papers at least, of sexual dysfunction. Gates sued McKenna for £250,000 pounds sterling. It was a nice try, but Gates ended up adding this lawsuit to the list of other things he lost to the amazing Mr. McKenna.[1]

But for Drs. Kroger, MacHovec, Crasilneck, et. al., there are inconvenient examples of misadventure within their own ranks of "licensed professionals." Dr. Dean Gerstenberger, an Arizona physician, gave a female subject the post-hypnotic suggestion she would forget the sexual advances he made upon her while she was in a trance.[2] She remembered anyway. There was Dr. Jules Masserman, Professor Emeritus of Neurology and Psychology at Northwestern University (Chicago), Honorary Professor for Life of the World Association of Social Psychiatry, and named "the most prominent psychiatrist in the world," with over four hundred published scientific papers. Dr. Masserman skipped the risky suggestion of post-hypnotic amnesia and went directly to injections of sodium amytal on five female patients, hoping that would erase their memory of his amorous assaults upon them.[3] It did not. Another "diplomate" was the Minnesota doctor who used a combination of hypnosis and sodium amytal to *create* a memory of *false* abuse that did *not* in fact occur and paid a court settlement of five-million-dollars to two patients.[4] But that didn't come close to the ten-million-dollar judgment against Dr. Bennett Braun at the prestigious Rush-Presbyterian-St. Luke's Medical Center in Chicago, who, through the power of suggestion, turned the mind of Patricia Burgus into a psychological rabbit farm, breeding three hundred different personalities, one of them a Satanic cannibal.[5]

---

1 *London Times*, July 14, 1998, p. 3; July 15, 1998, p. 3; July 16, 1998, p. 5; July 21, 1998, p. 3; July 22, 1998, p. 3; July 23, 1998, p. 3.
2 *Arizona Business Gazette*, June 24, 1993, p. 39.
3 *Chicago Tribune*, Nov. 10, 1987, sect. 3, p. 3.
4 staff.washington.edu/eloftus/Articles/sciam.htm
5 "Dangerous Therapy: The Story of Patricia Burgus and Multiple Personality Disorder," *Chicago Magazine*, June 1, 1998

The people who write my checks expect to see hypnotized people doing crazy things. They don't care if they actually go nuts in the process. All they care about is getting a *full show*. They don't want it shortened even if a subject slides into madness. No client has ever complained about an abreaction, only a show that doesn't go long enough. Weighing all the risks of turning one's sanity over to a floorshow hypnotist may have its dangers, according to Dr. Michael Heap writing in *Contemporary Hypnosis* (1995, no. 5), but no more than "many other everyday human activities" like skiing or hang gliding. It's unlikely a stage hypnotist will sexually molest anyone in a private manner in front of an audience, although there was a hypnotist in the college market known to whisper his motel room number to hypnotized females.

At the bar before my appearance one night, I sat next to a bearded man who said he was a licensed hypnotherapist on the faculty of the University of Minnesota. He did not recognize me as the evening's entertainment. In fact, he did not even know there *was* entertainment. All he came in for was a drink. Out of knavish sport I asked him his professional opinion of stage hypnotists. His lip muscles contracted and his eyes focused into the highball glass he clutched with both hands in a grip of strangulation.

"Many patients who could benefit from hypnotherapy," he said in a struggle with self-control, "do not seek it because they are afraid of being turned into a *goddam chicken!*" He told me about subjects in hypnosis shows who went into permanent emotional collapse. He said he had treated such cases. I asked the names of those hypnotists who did such harm, but he didn't know and said it didn't matter. In fact, he could not name a single stage hypnotist. Nor had he ever seen one perform. But "they should all be lined up and shot!" He sucked the rest of his highball down to the bottom and continued sucking in a loud gurgle. I can't say I disagreed. I imagined hundreds of competitors, the Great This, the Amazing That, the World's Only Whatever, Mystical Whoozits, Kings of Sleep, Sirens of Something, Zappers and Knock-Out Nolans, not to mention that Hypnotic Dog in Scotland—all eliminated. Except for myself, of course. I'd be the only exception.

"Why not," I said, "shove them in a pit and bury them *alive*, so they'd have a longer awareness of the full weight of judgment upon them?"

"Excellent idea!" His face lit up like day itself as he dug in his wallet to buy me a drink. We were joking, but not entirely.

Without telling him I was the entertainment, I arranged for him to see the show for free, saying I had a connection with the management. At least he'd have a better idea of what he hated. He was aghast when he saw me walk out on stage, but he stuck around anyway. To my surprise, he became caught up in the spectacle and laughed along with everyone else.

After the floor is cleared and the house lights turned back on, there are immediate questions people want answered. Why are my pants stuffed with newspaper? Why can't I remember what I did? Why is my scalp bleeding? To offer them something, I say that human consciousness is prone to the "funnel effect," a tendency to narrow itself down to just one thing to the exclusion of everything else, including so-called rational thought. It's why someone may focus their mind on a conspiracy website and end up believing the earth is controlled by lizard people. Why, in spite of all evidence to the contrary, do people believe that a presidential election was rigged and storm the US Capitol, urged on by a guy dressed up as a buffalo. I work the same proclivity by applying words in certain patterns (i.e. the "induction") known to penetrate the integument of "ordinary consciousness" and funnel it down into a trance. Once that's accomplished, I can rearrange the mental furniture any way I want. The more absurd the better. People nod their heads as if they understand, but in the end no question is ever really answered.

Skeptics simply scoff it off. The late James Randi, co-founder of the Committee for Skeptical Inquiry, asserted that hypnotic subjects are just "going along with it"[1] like André Breton's hypnotic mediums. When a screaming woman is wheeled away to the hospital unable to walk or unclench her fists, she's doing it, if we are to believe Randi, "to please the

---

1 Quoted by Michael Prescott,
michaelprescott.typepad.com/michael_prescotts_blog/2006/12/
hypnotized_by_s.html

hypnotist." With due regard to the skeptics, I might agree that stage hypnotism could be defined as the boldest public lie one can get away with.

But could that not be said of "reality" itself? Look at all the many interpretations of "baseline consciousness." Some people in India, supposedly not hypnotized, embrace the tradition of throwing their infants from the tops of religious shrines to the faithful below, who catch them like so many footballs.[1] Paul Theroux writes of young Plashwit men in Turkestan expected to honor their cultural tradition by traveling great distances while keeping a mouse alive inside their mouth. In parts of Ecuador, it's normal to feed cake and high denomination currency to donkeys at a festival until they throw up what is considered a sacred feast for humans.[2]

Is it possible in this jumble of realities that just one might somehow be the "real" reality and all the rest delusions? What do you call someone who believes in something you don't? Or vice versa? How real is going from town to town, annihilating people's "rational" selves on a stage under spotlights? Whatever it's called, if I do it *convincingly*, my enterprise stays in the black. If not, I'm liable to seek a living by even more ignoble means.

---

1 *New York Times,* July 28, 2016.
2 Paul Theroux, *Fresh Air Fiend* (2000), chap. "Unspeakable Rituals and Outlandish Beliefs."

II - Self

2 - Lounge Act Poet Blown Away

Footprints that met in the sand were erased
like their creators who are also erased
with the breeze of their absence.
—Yahuda Amichai (translated by Veronica Vixen)

I mentioned I would rather have been a poet. Actually, I was a poet. During the time I appeared onstage at the Canton Grill, the Dragon Lounge, Mr. Patrick's, the Red Bull, Tracy Star's, and the King of Hearts in Laramie (before it was shut down as a public nuisance), I was publishing poems in *Broken Streets*, *NewsArt*, *Fresh Air Magazine* and *Sunrise Review*. All the nightclub managers, pit drummers, exotic dancers and theatrical agents who knew me as a hypnotist would never have guessed that I sat in my motel room during the day composing free verse lyrics. They didn't know me as a poet because they didn't want to know me as a poet. In fact, they didn't want to know me at all. Since I'd be gone tomorrow, it was more convenient to think of me as just another entertainer with a flashy suit and a big mouth.

At the height of my poetic fame, I might have had as many as eight, possibly ten, serious readers. Friends, mostly. Or at least I thought they were friends. It's as difficult to maintain lasting friendships when you're on the road all the time as it is to be known as a poet solely on the basis of poems in small literary journals. Somewhat wider recognition might be gained at readings in local coffeehouses as long as you are populist and entertaining, but I didn't have that option. I had other people to please, and in that there was nothing poetic. Live audiences in night clubs shaped me much faster than the silent ones of invisible readers.

As an entertainer I lived under the hot metaphors of war. One night you kill, the next night you die. Working between dance sets at the Frontier Room in Vancouver or the Fantasia Cabaret in Edmonton, I *had* to "rip out their gizzard," as they say in stand-up slang, because if I didn't do it to them, they'd do it to me. My function, like those of others in my role (comics, magicians, ventriloquists) was to take up thirty minutes while dancers changed their gowns and break-away pantsuits. People were not there to see me. Since that's the life I lived, my poems were about what I knew, what I thought to be true, what I feared and what I dreamed. What I didn't realize was how foreign all of it was to anyone who did not live the same way I did, which was pretty much everyone.

It took three years of constant submissions before "Forced Landscape" was finally accepted by *Fault Line Review* and not a single known response from a single reader to the lines that echoed in my mind every night, "Is that my face / tacked upon the wall / and under foot upon the floor?" I should not be surprised at how perplexing "House Lights," "Massage Parlor Honeymoon," "Fist Patch," and "Spit Clown Dies in Fire" were to editors who opened the envelopes I sent them from all over the country. They must have thought I was trying to be frivolous, but I was not. Frivolity might have been the end result of my efforts on stage, but what went into my poems was urgently serious.

What could a mimeographed publication with a circulation of thirty, and a roadhouse that threw out that many on a good night possibly have in common? Rejection. Rejection slips said it all—"Sorry, not for us." As a performer, rejection came *after* the acceptance, that is, after I signed a contract with a theatrical agency on the usual basis of a week to get me in the door and the option to book a second week. If I wasn't good enough to make it through the first week, by the optional week I was out of there. "Sorry, not for us."

I simultaneously lived on opposite sides of a no-man's-land. On one side I was too estranged for poetry journals, and on the other I was not depraved enough for stripper 'n comic clubs. After a day of writing, I'd have to present myself to a club manager who'd say, "Gimme dick jokes, goddammit! Drag their ass through the gutter! That's why they're here. Pack this dump so I can make some money for a change!"

Contrary to what you hear, risqué laughs are not easy laughs. If you think they are, go down to open stage at your local comedy club and watch the amateurs give it a try. Tell me you can't feel the teeth of natural selection biting down. If the dirty joke fails, it not only doesn't get a laugh, it exposes something shameful about the teller that carries over to the next joke, making it more likely to fail too until a horrible smell fills the room and everyone knows where it's coming from. When you delve into the energies of the id you enter a labyrinth of forces and counter-forces that can either bring down the house, or implode into utter self-obliteration. But with the guts to face a crowd more than eager to eat you alive, you just *may,* with luck and sheer survival instinct, turn the tables and be the one who does the eating.

Cyril Connolly called them the "unsubdued daughters of Isis." I saw them in dressing rooms and I saw them on stage—the all-nude dancers. But I was under so much stress trying to *drag them through the gutter* (without soiling myself) that their talents were lost on me. But not on the older men, rich men, dangerous men, and slumming highbinders flush with cash and arrogance who always seemed to hang out in the places I worked. The daughters of Isis were attracted to the material provisioning and physical sensations they offered, the more intense the better—fast cars, private jets, outré sex, drugs, preferably all in combination. To the dancers, public and private were essentially the same. The route to what they wanted was direct and immediate. Like me, they were hired in one place just long enough to make an impression then off they'd go to somewhere else. It was easy to get into trouble and easy to leave it behind. But it wasn't without its risks. They were always in danger of sexual batteries of the he-said, she-said variety, and what sympathy could be expected by a loose woman in a community that didn't want her there in the first place? Every so often one went missing—or dead—but that did not discourage them. It was a risk they accepted and never thought it would happen to them. They were street savvy and not afraid to use whatever weapon they carried in their purse. My life was less festive, with fewer physical gratifications, but at least it was safer. And I had the sublime pleasure of art, whereas they did not.

One dancer who did not conform to this profile was Jenny Private. I'm changing her name to protect her privacy, but her stage name was equally preposterous. She traveled from club to club throughout the US and Canada with her mother, of all people, remaining not so much aloof as oblivious to the offstage capers of her fellow entertainers. From what I could tell, burlesque dancers often did not have a good relationship with their parents, but in Jenny's case I could only marvel at such a mother-daughter closeness. Jenny was as naïve as any sheltered girl and could not open her mouth without showing it. How she got into this line of work at all, much less in collaboration with her mother, was a mystery, but probably no more than how I—or any of us—got into it. We all had our personal stories and no one asked any questions.

For two weeks I, Jenny, and her mother shared a mobile home parked behind the Kin Tiki, a notorious roadhouse on a windswept stretch of land between Spokane and Coeur d'Alene. Several other dancers shared the trailer too. After our contracts with the club were up, we'd all be moving on to a similar situation elsewhere. As was often the case, I acted as a breakwater between the women and all the shifty male traffic that sloshed through the place. Late at night, if there was a knock at the door, I was the one expected to answer it. If it was some creep no one was expecting, I turned him away. If it was some creep they *were* expecting, I let him in. The Privates took no part in that. The only thing they were a part of was each other.

There was a common area in front of the trailer, but since everyone was transient, no one bothered to keep it tidy—except for Jenny and her mother. They made it a kind of home and it was where I did my reading and wrote my poems. Whenever they started a conversation with me, they were really talking with each other, and I was just a transparent screen between them. They were that way with everyone, and the other dancers barely hid their derisive smirks, which I doubt the Privates even noticed. They were like flat stones skipping over water from one thing to another, then something else again, and again and again. First it was cotton thread, then brands of hairspray, then all the times Jenny had seen penguins at a zoo. She loved penguins so much that she wanted to have one. Her mother encouraged her. She said in all seriousness she wanted to go to Antarctica and *be* a penguin. Her mother supported that too. Then it was musicals and movie stars and dreams of the future, lots of dreams, and more dreams, opportunities, and overnight fame and living in Hollywood right under the famous sign. They talked about a sister, a "daddy," a farm, all in the past tense, but something ominous seemed to have happened that was never specified, and that might have been the key to why they were doing what they were doing. Jenny's mother wanted to know all about my family, why my parents got divorced and how much alimony my father paid, what relatives on each side of the family thought about it, and which parent I sided with and why. Each question seemed to hint at the unsaid event in their past. When I said my father was a magician who had been on TV and worked through the same agency that booked Bob Hope, Mrs. Private asked if he could introduce them to the famous comedian and get Jenny into a movie, preferably a musical. She asked me how much money I made and for some reason I felt I had to go along with their fantasizing, so I gave a ridiculous figure which she believed without question. As they spoke, I wrote a lyric about them that ended, "in a room without a door / yet with one, / lives the kiss / a house of air and wish."

One thing I never saw in nightclubs was anyone rehearsing. That would include myself. Hypnotism is something that cannot be practiced alone in front of a mirror. So rehearsal and show coincide. Whatever routines a dancer had were repeated so many times on a nightly basis that there was nothing left to practice. Other things were more important, like the pursuit of personal thrills. Jenny was different. She and her mother had higher hopes, so Jenny practiced new dance moves every day in hopes of being noticed by someone who would offer her a fabulous career opportunity.

I remember the time one afternoon I sat writing in their presence. Jenny went into their large bedroom and came out in a red sequined robe hemmed with fake white fur. It was held by a single snap at the neck and open the rest of the way down. Underneath she was in her underwear. It was no surprise to me because onstage I'd seen her enough times in considerably less. Her mother helped her gather it up in a couple of places and secure it with pins. Then she put on some music and Jenny began dancing, making spins and turns that rocked the flimsy trailer. The robe spread open in a revealing way, but that was not a concern to either of them.

"Which looks better," she asked me, "this way or this way?"

Every move and swish of the robe revealed, as intended, her plump flesh jiggling in shallow waves, but not intended to be arousing. This was only practice. With all her vigorous activity Jenny began to smell of sweat, perfume, and a faint something I associated with livestock. The only concern in her universe was the exactness of her footwork, as if any of the customers at the Kon Tiki really cared. I realized with each passing moment that she was as lost as lost could be. I wrote, "...a delicacy that burns to live / within her shell's hard sky."

She demonstrated other talents like touching the tip of her nose with her tongue, and bending her hand back so her fingernails were flat against her forearm. She rotated her head so her chin touched her shoulder bone. She flared her nostrils in and out, wiggled her ears, and alternately lifted each eyebrow as if it were pulled up by a string. Her mother regarded these stunts as pure talent. Fortunately, she did not work them into her dance routine. Onstage she didn't "sell sex," a phrase used all the time by club managers to assess the value of each dancer. Liquored-up cat-calling was part of what made these places work, and the dancers encouraged it in various ways, but in Jenny's case she ignored it. As a result, the cat-calling took on a hostile edge, as if they wanted to force out of her something she wasn't giving them. Yet she did have an odd, almost comic appeal, which attracted the attention of an occasional docile, older man who would give her a hefty tip. Maybe he felt sorry for her or felt that she, but for the grace of

God, could be his own daughter. Some of the dancers did the innocent girl routine, but it was an act. Jenny's childlike innocence was not an act. She actually was an innocent lamb and it seemed like only a matter of time before somehow, somewhere, the wolves would get her.

Late one night as everyone was asleep, there was a knock at the trailer door and in my role as gatekeeper I answered it. A heavy-set older man in a suit, apparently intoxicated, asked for Jenny by name. I said she wasn't here and the man went away looking so crushed I wondered whether he was just another nut or someone from her unmentioned past.

Eventually, as I expected, Jenny's mother asked if I could hypnotize her to dance better. Off stage sessions were the last thing I wanted since there was no money or glory in it. I was in somewhat of a bind because every night Mrs. Private cooked up a hodgepodge of a dinner from food left behind by others, while Jenny chattered on about agencies, clubs, Hollywood, and Bob Hope's movies. So out of obligation I gave in and agreed. I applied the conventional procedure of progressive relaxation but could not determine the degree her conscious state had changed except by what I could infer through her slackening facial expression, slumped posture, and labored breathing. As I began a series of suggestions, I realized her mother was slumped over too, and reacting exactly as her daughter. When I told Jenny her arm was levitating upward, her mother's arm also rose. When I said she could not lift her arm, it remained down, as did her mother's. *Your body will move by instinct, and you'll feel the music in every muscle. Nod your head if you understand.* Jenny nodded her head, and so did her mother. I gave her suggestions that just as well could have applied to myself. *And as this happens, you will show the audience just a—*I searched for the word—*whiff of contempt, like you are going to please them on your own terms. Taunt them with it. Don't overdo it, because it's a strong spice. Just a little contempt so it doesn't look like you are trying too hard. Make them come to you.*

When I told her to open her eyes, her mother opened her eyes at the same time and they both gazed around with identical looks of bedazzlement. That obligation was out of the way. I didn't notice any change in the way she danced.

On a Saturday, the usual start day for new acts, the agency sent out a dancer named Veronica Vixen. She was thin and small-breasted for a dancer, with black hair pulled back in a twist. She wore black-buckled ankle boots and a long, gray dress with a matching silk shawl. Her skin was pale and she wore only a minimum of eyeliner. When she introduced herself, she spoke with what seemed to be a speech defect. Where Jenny was open with no defenses, Veronica was guarded as a wild animal. Her eyes scanned everywhere, not in a quick way, but in slow intense sweeps, as if looking for danger. She regarded each of us no longer than necessary, the Privates with indifference, me with apprehension.

That night, leading up to showtime, we sat at a coffee table before Mrs. Private's not altogether unpalatable meal. Veronica put a few scraps on her plate but didn't eat any of it. She stared at me, trying to figure out how I fit into all this. Her contributions to the conversations, labored because of something wrong with her tongue, came after long intervals, as if every word had to pass through stations of weighed assessment. She allowed nothing, no matter how small, to take her unawares. Afterward, while getting ready, Jenny and her mother broke into song from some musical, then discussed between themselves whether a penguin could outrun a tornado. Veronica observed all this, saying nothing. During a pause in the chatter, I leaned toward her and, to place myself in a different context, said, "night walks, scattering poems." I wasn't expecting anything from this, so I was surprised when in reply she struggled back slowly but clear enough to be understood, "The dark still nurses its secret." Thus began my poetic relationship with an audience of one.

The Privates yakked and laughed away in their own world, while Veronica expressed to me, one slow word at a time, her appreciation for Sylvia Plath (whom she initially quoted), Marianne Moore, Wallace Stevens, Sylvia Townsend Warner, Hilda Doolittle, Louise Bogan, Robert Lowell. She recognized my quote from Cummings, but wrote off his work as merely cute. She said that Ginsberg wrote a few masterpieces that captured a certain mode of living, but was primarily a cult figure too embedded in his times. She asked me what I thought of Marianne Moore's use of hyphens (I had no idea) and Elizabeth Bishop's knots of stresses (something I never thought about). She wondered, since Moore and Bishop were friends, whether they tried to outdo each other in the use of colors. Which did I think was more refined, Bishop's amethyst as a quality of sand grains, or Moore's use of the same color as a quality of jellyfish? Did they have some kind of signal going between them when Bishop described the top of a fir tree as a turkey foot, and Moore described the same thing as a fish spine? It was beyond what I knew. Her words, distortedly pronounced as if in some foreign accent, so captivated me that later, onstage, when she indeed "sold sex," and plenty of it, to the audience, all I saw was something tragic.

In the following days and nights, while the other dancers came and went with assorted men (or women, or couples), Veronica and I found ourselves in the front of the trailer unavoidably with Jenny and her mother. Veronica made trips out to her car, and when she came back, her eyes looked like plastic and her speech even more slurred than before, as if she had a rock in her mouth. This was when I first suspected her speech impediment had something to do with what she did in the car. I read her a poem about troubled sleep and the boogeyman, and compared it to Richard Wilbur's "claws / Of nightmare flap you pathless God knows where..." She answered with Plath's "I am inhabited by a cry. / Nightly it flaps out / Looking, with its hand, for something to love." I read two of the three parts of my "Ode to Lola Capri," of which the third part included the lines: "he was mechanical failure / with his yes, his yes indeed / he was the wrong answer / passing signs that groaned in winds of not-to-be/ singing, singing loudly / Lola, Lola Capri." Veronica said *things* were more reliable than people, citing Genevieve Taggard, "...arts and trinkets...never played me false... / They lasted til you came, then / When you went, sufficed again."

I asked her she if she'd ever felt that betrayed.

In slow motion she said, "Five years ago." Then said no more.

When Jenny and her mother were present, I made a feeble attempt to include them in our talk. Jenny's mother asked if poets made a lot of money. I told her yes, some of them were fabulously rich and she believed it. Eventually they dropped out of the conversation altogether. For a while they hovered about like two aimless bees around a hive that had just been removed. Then they went back to the bedroom in the back of the trailer and played a tape of *Oklahoma* over and over again. I could hear mother and daughter talking and laughing and singing for what seemed like the rest of the night.

In a rare moment alone with Veronica, I initiated a session of old-fashioned necking and was taken aback by how oddly arid she was. Her mouth was a kiln, and her hair could have been the wig on a mannequin. I slipped my hand to where I felt skin dry as the fabric that covered it. In the process of discovering how elusive her tongue was, like some wounded beast hiding in a cave, she disclosed to me "heroin is better than sex." That explained what she did in her car. She explained that visible needle marks would be unseemly on her exposed body, so she did her injections under the tongue. Sheer youth maintained her physical appearance for the time being, but there was no telling when collapse would set in. All we could share was our respective solitudes, and on the basis of that we settled in to a mutually dependent friendship where I was a different kind of audience as she read aloud with her self-inflicted speech defect my "Banana Neck," an allegory of fake confidence, ("As if that slap / of another hope / would make something click"). And "Sailor Boy" ("I'm a ship of fire / plunging over the edge / of her flat earth").

Not surprisingly, Veronica was held over another week at the Kon Tiki and, in spite of some disastrously failed performances, so was I. Jenny Private, regardless of my hypnotizing her to dance better, was not. I looked forward to her and her mother being gone, but before they left, Jenny flew out of their bedroom in flannel pj's printed with little penguins and pulled me aside. She begged me to tell her, "What does 'contempt' mean?" I don't know what I told her, but I wished her well and after that I never saw her or her mother again.

Not all nightclub managers demanded I work blue. Most were happy I simply show up on time and sober enough not to fall off the stage. But there was still the pressure, direct or indirect, for me to *drag them through the gutter.* The language of the gutter came easily to a lot of people around me, but in my case, I had to do it consciously and with forethought. The trick was to make it sound natural, and then apply it to my performance. I had already gotten to the point where I could hypnotize people on a stage often enough to claim legitimacy, but carrying it to the point of "dragging their ass through the gutter" was another matter altogether. That was a skill I was forced to find the secret to. As a person of books, where else could I turn but to them?

I'd already discovered that if a hypnotism how-to book was listed in a library catalogue, it was usually stolen off the shelf, an indication of how valuable the secret was. Bookstores, new and used, didn't carry books on stage hypnotism, only the how-it-can-help-you type of dreck, so I resorted to search services, paying inflated prices for books sent to me care of General Delivery at scheduled mail drops. In the front of small-town post offices, I sat in my car and eagerly tore open packages of what I hoped would be what I was looking for. I received an ancient, falling-apart copy of *25 Lessons in Hypnotism* (no date) by L. E. Young, with the cover illustration of a man with lightning bolts coming out his bulging eyes and one hand raised toward the breast of a mesmerized woman. I inhaled its chapters on "How to Hypnotize a Room Full at One Time," "How to Put Your Subject into a Six Days' Trance," and "How to Make Money Out of Hypnotism," but only found comments like "command them to hold their eyes absolutely in this position and not let the eyeballs fall," or "tell them that it will only be a few seconds until they will feel drowsy and sleepy, and the desire for sleep will take possession of their whole bodies," or "no matter how hard it is to influence a subject, if you persist and he does not resist, you will succeed at last." No help there. *Hypnotism for Professionals* (1953) by Konradi Leitner was the cost of a lavish dinner, but all it provided was lame advice like "your manner should be that of an efficient orchestra conductor." *Dr. Herbert L. Flint's Hypnotic Routine* (circa 1897) described his toothache stunt, electrocution and other "horrible exhibitions," but no specifics on how to make them happen, especially in a bar full of hecklers. Ormond McGill's *Encyclopedia of Stage Hypnotism*

(1953), mentioned pumping ether into the subject's face through a tube concealed in the sleeve, or using the "Bulldog Method" where you grab the subject by the throat and squeeze until he collapses. The sheer aggression of this last method had its appeal, but I was not about to try it.

The trunk of my car filled up with the writings of William Cook ("a false assumption of self-confidence is quickly realized by others"), Professor Leonidas ("look at a button for three minutes"), Edward Eldridge ("in hypnotism the first thing to be done is to secure a suitable subject"), Harry Arons ("A nightclub is hardly the kind of setting the hypnotist would choose"), Peter Diamond ("you cannot hypnotize people under the influence of drugs or alcohol"), Franquin ("the rebellion of his moral personality would make itself felt so strongly that the hypnotic influence would be ineffectual"), Palmer-Jones ("hypnotize a subject and have *him* call *you* the next day after lunch, perhaps after eating spinach if you know he dislikes spinach"), L. W. De Laurence ("take any ordinary steel hat pin and in force it through his cheek"). It was all the same: cheaply printed, yellowing pages and alluring covers with comely females succumbing to mesmeric control. Carl Sextus, L. W. De Laurence, Dr. S. J. van Pelt, Louis Schlathoelter, and all the others, described techniques and various outrages to inflict on hapless volunteers, but nothing, absolutely *nothing* specific on how to "*drag their ass through the gutter*" in such a way as to keep a nightclub manager off my back.

My first breakthrough came not from reading anything in a book but by witnessing someone who practiced what I was increasingly pressured to do. It was at the Dunes in Las Vegas that I saw the Great Maurice. (I'm changing his name because his son, who has taken up the trade, knows who I am and is known to break things.) Before showtime, the stage was set with a row of chairs facing the audience and downstage center was a mic stand and microphone with a ludicrous gold-plated head shining in the spotlight. A three-piece combo played intro music and then a fanfare for someone in his fifties wearing a coal-black tux perfectly cut to his corpulent body as he majestically strode onto the stage projecting the ultimate in manly, big-cigar triumphalism.

From the moment he seized the gold-plated mic, obscenity flowed from his lips as smoothly as a sermon from the pulpit. He claimed that hypnosis could cure just about anything (like drinking and gambling, laugh, laugh) and if you let him put you under, he'd give you "a shitload of good luck" at the tables before you went back to your room for some "kick-ass whoop-de-do" followed by "the best night's sleep you ever fucking had." Volunteers wasted no time rushing up on stage.

He warned anyone with ideas of trying to sabotage the proceedings that they better leave the stage immediately before they were discovered and exposed, or the results "would not be pretty." No one left. He told everyone to concentrate on him (which they were doing before they walked in the door), then, in a tone evocative of religious ritual, went into a long incantation suggesting sleep. During this phase he held off on the obscenities. As the subjects all sat transfixed, he approached a middle-aged man in a Hawaiian shirt, clasped him by the back of the neck and literally hurled him to the floor, yelling the word "Sleep!" At the sound of tourist bones hitting the stage, everyone gasped and knew the Great Maurice meant business. The reaction caused one female subject to open her eyes at which point Maurice unceremoniously kicked her off the stage. The next victim was a woman in her forties wearing a short party dress. Maurice shoved her head down between her knees as he shouted "Sleep!" She slowly slipped off her chair and dropped like a dead person, her dress hiking up so you could see her underpants. People in the back of the room stood for a better look. Soon enough they would see a whole lot more. He continued pulling people out their seats until he had them dragged into a pile like a Boston lobster harvest, then came forward for a glorious bow.

Each stunt that followed escalated to the next in an ascending order of outrage. He made them furnish the sound track for a porno movie, do a sex pill testimonial, leap in the air when imaginary dildos shot up through the seat of their chairs, and conducted a simulated orgy with inflatable male and female dolls. For ninety minutes this tuxed monster, with his gold-plated microphone like a war club, dominated his volunteers in an exultance of pure will. There was no humiliation too extreme, no gutter too foul. His big finale was planting the hypnotic command that they were all—male and female alike— striptease dancers peeling off their clothes. They exposed breasts, pubes and testicles while the combo played "The Stripper" by the David Rose Orchestra. The audience went out of control. In *Laughing and Crying, a Study of the Limits of Human Behavior* (1941) Helmuth Plessner argued that the terminal end of laughter is a boundary situation of embarrassment and despair that extracts maximum power the nearer it gets to the darkness of the tragic.

I tried to determine whether these people were really under some kind of mesmeric influence or just too intimidated to resist. At first I thought his more dramatic subjects might even be accomplices, but concluded they were acting out some kind of exhibitionistic need. I couldn't be sure. Maybe it wasn't hypnosis or even entertainment at all, but a throwback to something ancient and primal tricked out as a stage show. I never imagined someone could be applauded for such effrontery. If there was anything to be learned it was how willingly people will allow themselves to be degraded, and how enthusiastically it could be received by onlookers.

When it was over, volunteers left the stage and were mobbed by the curious. *Do you remember humping the sheep? Do you remember pulling down your pants? Do you remember anything?*

Maurice detached and slipped the gold-plated microphone into the front pocket of his tuxedo pants with practiced ease so no one would steal it when he wasn't looking, and made himself available at the bar. He pulled the knot from his bow tie and let the ends hang down each side of a ruffled shirt soaked in sweat. This dissipated-looking tyrant, with the pale, pudgy face of someone who lived for years on rail drinks and bar food, had no lack of women admirers. He rubbed some of the stage make-up from around his thinning hairline with a napkin, leaving a few bits of tissue clinging to his wet temple. One of his female minions devotedly picked them off. After downing a shot of tequila, he set the glass gently on the bar and gestured for another. His motions were all highly controlled and occurred at about three fourths normal speed, which had the effect of making me focus on him even more, something I'm sure he was aware of because, without looking at me, said, "You wanna ask me something, dontcha?"

I did. I couldn't come right out and ask, *What's the trick to dragging people through the gutter*? Instead, I went about it more indirectly by asking what he thought of William James's theory of the mind's function for ends that may not exist in the world of sensory impressions. I queried as to what extent he might have relied on that theory to cause a man in the audience to jump to his feet on a posthypnotic command and yell, "I'm Tinkerbell, the biggest fairy in Vegas!"

He stared at me and said nothing, then downed another shot of tequila and gestured for another.

I tried to keep momentum by citing Morton Prince's theories of multiple personality where consciousness is divided by walls of amnesia, comparing that to Ernest Hilgard's theory of divided consciousness. I even brought up Kant's "Copernican hypothesis," which proposes that necessary truths are relative to the standpoint of the observer. I asked Maurice if he used that as a basis for the stunt to get a female subject to throw her underwear into the audience.

His only reply was, "That's what I thought. You're out to steal whatever you can."

There was a pause in which I could have said something but I had nothing more to say.

"When you walk out on that stage everything you just told me doesn't mean shit." He took the gold-plated mic from his pocket and held it in front of my face. "You know what this is?"

"A microphone?"

He let out a long sigh and wrinkled his gray brows darkened with pencil.

"I'll give you a hint." He lowered it down to crotch level.

"OK, a penis."

"A penis! What are you, a fucking nurse? It's your cock, pinhead, your goddam *prick*! You walk out there with your prick in your hand and wave it around like you know what to do with it. Then you *fuck* em through every hole in their head!"

"Yes, sir, I understand."

He slumped his shoulders in a gesture of exaggerated deflation. "No you don't."

44

Maybe I didn't. But in a way maybe I did. Perhaps he told me everything I needed to know.

There was still too much of the scribe in me. As a poet who valued the shadow weight of a single word, I found profanity excessively laden. I associated it with the kind of people I was supposed to be dragging through the gutter, people with whom I had nothing in common. It was why I had to construct a whole new personality. I bought a tape recorder and read aloud from newspapers and advertisements, improvising vulgarities, then listened to how it sounded. Hearing my own voice so much out of character was ludicrous. But I made myself do it. I developed a repertoire of obscenities, then started putting them to use. I learned that to the extent I showed any uncertainty, any hesitation, my listeners sensed it. They knew I was not legit and treated me accordingly. It was in the heat of this battle that I quickly evolved.

Freud claimed that "tendentious jokes" (the dirty ones) had to be made without showing any sign of enjoying (or not enjoying) them, as it would interfere with their cathectic "discharge" (laughter[1]). Since that "discharge" is based on the release of a constrained energy, a certain inhibition has to be maintained. This was the difficult part—to hold back and to release at the same time.

My early experiments were perfect examples of failure, but once I learned to set up suggestions with the necessary maintenance of inhibition, they began to succeed. Exquisite care had to be taken in suggesting the Penis Enlargement Testimonial. I could not flat out suggest it, as that would deny the inhibitory component. I had to frame the suggestion in terms of conservation of energy: *You invented the device and it made you rich! You have every right to be arrogant!* According to Freud, those witnessing such a situation possess a "readiness for inhibition" which, when breached, results is that sought-for discharge of laughter. In those dark nights of the soul following an especially awful failure at trying to be obscene, I considered going into some other line of work, but all I came up with was

---

1 *Jokes and their Relation to the Unconscious* (1905), Chap. V, "The Motives of Jokes—Jokes as a Social Process," especially pp. 106-115.

poet. Like the dancers, I was in a life that offered no better alternatives. So, I stayed where I was and kept struggling.

On weekends there were more couples in the audience and therefore more female volunteers, but women made tricky subjects in the blue zone. For deep subconscious reasons, even in places like the Kon Tiki, audiences would not accept a woman being ridiculed as ruthlessly as a man. It was always open season on men, but not women. I figured out that one way to get around the problem was through gender reversal, as in Maurice's Woman with a Wanker routine. A hypnotized woman acting like a man trying to pick up a woman (played by a man) had that elusive quality that Freud called "unanswerableness" necessary to provoke laughter. If I asked the female subject (posing as a man) *What do women like about you?* they did not need to exercise much imagination to play the man as sexual fool. They knew the routine quite well already.

By trial and sometimes quite painful error, I worked with subjects, audiences and especially myself to put together a more or less acceptable X-rated hypnotic performance. The best stunts were those that were self-perpetuating, like the Sex Reversal, the Penis Enlargement Testimonial, and the Pregnant Man. Rehearsal and show continued conterminously. As one of Freud's votaries, Lou Andreas-Salomé, wrote, analyst and subject together "quench their thirst from the same well, like the animals of the desert that meet at the same oasis."

In addition to the usual riffraff, I began to notice a different kind of person in my audiences—men in business suits, medical types still in scrubs, married couples, gray-haired women in pairs who did not take off their coats. They were not there because of the dancers. They had seen the word "hypnotist" in newspaper ads for the club and were willing to sit through sets of slinky Jezebels and their hooting fans in order to satisfy their curiosity about something else. They approached me afterward with questions as incongruous as their presence, questions of a psychological, metaphysical, even spiritual nature. Could I hypnotize someone in secret and make that person tell the truth? Could I reveal who they were in a previous incarnation? Could I make them remember their childhood? Could I make someone forget someone? Could I contact the dead? Could I make a crippled person walk? If there was any value to what I did, here was my opportunity to redeem it. But I did not. After desultory answers to their deep questions, I went back to my room to write poems and forgot about them entirely.

With this came a change in my poetry. I went from a few readers to no readers. The time I could have spent helping someone remember their childhood I spent composing "Pay at The Gate," "Song of Last Chances" and "The Tuneout." "Pecker Pinball" was accepted by *Telepoem* and read in Homeric oral tradition on their answering machine message for anyone compelled to call, but I didn't want to pay the long-distance charge to hear it and probably no one else did either. I picked up my rejections at post offices care of General Delivery all over the country, always leaving a forwarding address to a town six weeks ahead. I missed some pickups and for all I know there might have been poems published without my knowledge. The acceptance notice for "Full Moon," the personification of some infernal entity who "appears on a napkin / with razor and rage / then recedes / to appear in the notebooks / of a whiskered queen," finally reached me somewhere in Nevada with so many forwardings that they started using the back of the envelop.

As I crawled along the peeler circuit in social isolation, it was gratifying to go into a post office and find, amidst all the "sorry not for us" rejection slips, a letter from Veronica written in pencil on lined paper. But if I was in Laredo, she'd be in Spokane. If I was in Spokane, she'd be in Whitehorse. If I was in Kamloops, she'd be in Edmonton. All this separation inspired me to write the "Love Long Distance" series beginning with "He rubbed the pane / clear enough to see through / and groped in blackchance to form her breathing." We both might have preferred a more meaningful relationship, but knew it was not possible. She strung me along as a refreshing alternative to something that did not involve addiction (which she talked about kicking someday), and I compartmentalized her into a Beatrice for poetic purposes. In local libraries or gift shops I managed to meet the occasional farm girl, waitress or school teacher who found me interesting to correspond with for a while, but soon enough they realized it was not going to lead anywhere and they stopped writing.

During a layover in Las Vegas, I was wandering through the Dunes tricked out like any two-bit lounge act when I had the good fortune to meet a wonderful patron, the elegant and elderly Louise N. Johnson of St. Paul, Minnesota. She was a living chandelier, covered with massive drippages of clacking jewelry hanging from skeletal arms she could barely raise to pat an intricately structured pompadour. Through her thick bifocals she could spot a poet across the floor of any casino. As I passed her at the bar, she reached out a bony claw and snagged me by the sleeve.

"Young man," she said in a raspy voice that indicated some drastic procedure done to her larynx, "you look like a million dollars in twenty-dollar bills."

"Costume," I said. "All costume."

"I think there's got to be more to *this* story. Here, sit down."

Behind her unprepossessing appearance with all the plumage and coloration to conceal her age and infirmities was an artistic temperament. Beyond my own concealments she saw a poet desperate to be read. It was a fortuitous meeting because she happened to write the Poetry Corner in the *Sun Newspaper* distributed free door to door in the Twin Cities suburbs. She understood my frustration trying to write for poetry journals that found me as inscrutable as a native from the rainforest. She said she knew other poets in the same dilemma whose names were as unrecognizable to me as mine would be to them. And she knew them *personally*. This dear creature in her final years, fortressed as she was behind layers of disguise, became my savior. I left a packet of my poems with her. A few weeks later she devoted one of her columns to me under the headline, "Poetry That Confuses, Then Stimulates."[1]

In the middle of winter, I accepted her invitation to read at a poetry conclave in Minneapolis. I drove non-stop from Wyoming to be in a lineup of local poets associated with the

---

1 *Sun Newspapers*, Minneapolis, Minnesota, Jan. 25, 1978.

Loft Literary Society. It was a blizzardy night, yet a surprising number of people showed up, including the incomparable Mrs. Johnson. A soft-spoken young man with greasy hair recited an ode to a tree house. A woman dressed in black read a moving description of a garden overgrown after her grandmother's death. A creative writing teacher in a gray beard electrified the room with a series of lyrics on farm life, ending with one about a collapsed cow revived by jumping on its body to force out a quantity of blocked gas. Each poet received enthusiastic applause and I enjoyed them all for being so different from what I was used to. When it was my turn, I read the poem I dedicated to Mrs. Johnson, "House of Rented Dreams," ending with, "a world of answers / all coming together / as the house explodes." Silence. When I read "Face Focus Burnhole" there was an even more silent silence. When I closed with "Massage Parlor Honeymoon," the only response was one faint "tsk" to the lines, "Wallets opened and closed / In that bitter vicarage, / Wasting secrets like money / in a sandstorm of laughter."

I left the podium (no applause). When the session was over no group clustered around me as they did with the others. A little too hastily I thanked Mrs. Johnson and left the building, left town entirely. I had no home to return to so there was no point sticking around. I plunged my filthy entertainer's car through encroaching finger drifts and honked away jackrabbits on the long haul to Laramie where my next engagement was at the King of Hearts. Because I was in the business of applause, and sensitive to the lack of it, I spent the entire night in my capsule behind the wheel thinking about the other poets and all the applause, even cheers, they received. Was I the only one who saw congruence between the tree house ode and my own "House of Rented Dreams"? Why did they bestow hosannas on the poet of the flatulent cow, but my "biggest misunderstanding / That ever straddled his Sunday" in "Massage Parlor Honeymoon" was met with no reaction at all? Maybe I had the wrong wardrobe (I agree, it wasn't the occasion to look like a million dollars in twenty-dollar bills), or the wrong attitude (like the one I'd been carefully cultivating), or maybe I didn't know anyone in town and couldn't paper the house with applauding friends. Maybe my poems didn't deal with any kind of experience anyone could relate to. Or maybe they were just plain bad.

In the world of poetry, I searched for the highest truths. On stage I searched for the lowest. The more expert I became at degrading eager volunteers for laughs, the less appealing were my poems about smashed toilet stalls and bugs buzzing around motel signs. The number of people who reacted to the Heat Seeking Dildo, the Man from Nantucket, and the Inflatable Woman Testimonial vastly exceeded those who read "The Tuneout," "Song of Last Chances," and "Channels of Want." I became a saleable commodity at the Shelly Rae, Dave Sobel and Holly Hills agencies, among others, and my salary went from one fourth that of an ecdysiast to almost a third. I drank the milk of an alien paradise.

In the realm of poetry not only did I earn nothing, but my themes became ever more incomprehensible to anyone except a stage performer, all of whom were dedicated non-readers. The last poem I published, "Chuckhole," appeared in Mrs. Johnson's poetry column and ended, "my last words / an old billboard / torn apart by wind."

When the news of her death finally caught up with me at General Delivery during another layover in Las Vegas, I drove all the way out on the strip in the middle of the night, past the MGM, the Mirage, the Stratosphere, then past the "adult" motels and the old downtown, then further out, past block after block of smaller and seedier casinos claiming bigger payouts, until they gave way to alcoholic dives, last chance gas stations, salvage yards and finally the darkness of the desert under light-polluted stars. I stood at the edge of a pale-yellow nimbus over a shack of wheel rims and hubcaps and marked my transition from poet to barroom hypnotist by letting the wind carry my unwanted poems to their final oblivion like the ashes of someone you can't live without.

3 - Sway Back

Since I'm paid to be a public influence, it's not in my interest to shun anyone. In fact, I need all the people I can get and it doesn't matter how. I know nothing about who these people might be and they know nothing about me. We all work from a clean slate. I arrive in town a stranger with no past, no future, and I leave that way. I exist only as a short-lived spectacle.

In a typical week I might drive from Minneapolis to Newton, Iowa for a high school assembly, then to the Hotel Ft. Des Moines the same night to ridicule a dozen "good sports" at the state convention of Iowa Athletic Directors, leave my car at the Des Moines airport the next morning, fly to Phoenix, rent a car, rush up to Prescott for a show at Yavapai Community College, leave the next morning for a noon teaser and evening show at Mesa Community College, drive the next morning to Globe for a 1:30 p.m. assembly program and then immediately drive to Cochise Community College in Douglas for an 8 p.m. performance, after which I take a flight back to Des Moines, pick up my car, drive to Club 151 outside Anamosa for an evening show, drive all night to Sioux City for a morning assembly program, then immediately drive home to Minneapolis, pick up my mail, send out new contracts, sleep an hour, then do an after dinner presentation at the Radisson Hotel for two hundred cardiac surgeons looking for "something different."

To the extent that I control people for the amusement of others, there are those who control me for reasons of their own. Since what I do is for the purpose of generating attention, it has the side effect of attracting certain individuals who want to divert that attention to themselves. It's unavoidable and something that's never mentioned in hypnotism how-to books. The phenomenon does appear in medical and psychiatric literature under the category "somatoform and functional somatic syndromes," where an impairment is presented for purposes of manipulation. It's been estimated that fifteen to twenty-percent of primary care patients fall into this "all in your head" category[1]. That percentage seems to carry over to me.

By making hypnotism the topic *de jour*, those to whom I make myself available tell me their experiences with it good or bad. How they quit smoking, gave a painless birth, overcame their fear of dentist fingers. I'm obliged to hear the failures too. How they're still fat, still smoke, still bite their nails. If I'm going to expect strangers to play along with me, it's only reasonable that I play along with them. There is no reception desk between me and the public, so I am wide open to all the lures. Like any social contract, if something is offered, something is expected. What I offer is on stage. What is offered to me is in private. My influence is carefully planned, sometimes even written out in advance, but the influence of others is spontaneous, subconscious, like a child who manipulates a parent. And the parent can encourage that manipulation unawares.

At a place I'll call the Follies outside of Portland (I can't remember the actual place) I was talking to a few people as usual after one of my demonstrations. Standing aside was a tall redhead with wide hips and a long neck. That, with her high hair, made her resemble an ostrich. When she finally had me to herself, she said, "Someone wants to talk to you." She led me over to a table but no one was there. We sat and chatted about nothing in particular and I began to suspect this other "someone" did not exist. I'd seen the gambit before. It was an effective way to pin me down while the groundwork for something else could be laid. If the promised "someone" were a female, and at some other location, that would be a red flag for me to back away. There were those who knew that entertainers

---

1 James C. Hamilton, Ph.D., Marc D. Feldman, M.D., & Alan J. Cunnien, M.D., *Factitious Disorders in Medical and Psychiatric Practices* (2018), Chapter 8.

could have jaded tendencies as well as carry more cash than the average person.

I had a cousin who unfortunately could not see the red flag. He was a doctor on the surgical teaching staff at the Medical College of Ohio. While in Chicago for a medical convention he decided to go by himself one night to Rush Street, an area known for its strip clubs and prostitutes. According to news reports he left one of the clubs, leaving his coat behind even though the temperature outside was eighteen degrees. The next time he was seen was the following morning in an alley behind the club. Dead. Three stories up, a window was open. He either fell or was thrown out.[1] Someone had to have lured him up to the third-floor room, but beyond that no other details were ever discovered. A perfect murder. Whatever lured him to that third-floor room is unknown, but if the intention was robbery, something went terribly wrong, because when he was found he had $83 dollars in his wallet. My father liked to bring up the incident as a cautionary tale. "Don't get into anything you can't get out of."

"Franny is in the ladies' room," the woman said as she shook out a cigarette and let it lay on the table in front of her. "It's been a while, so she's probably throwing up a ball of hair."

This was another red flag—involvement with someone else's problems. I didn't ask any questions because I didn't want to show any interest. The redhead with the cigarette sensed this, so she changed the subject.

"How did you start doing what you do?"

"I read an ad on a matchbook."

I let this sarcasm serve as discouragement. She looked down at the cigarette in front of her. "I know a few things about hypnotists. I see their shows whenever they come through this way. They're all adrenaline junkies and aren't happy unless they're pushing things right up to the point of disaster. They make a lot of money, though. I'll give them that."

---

1 "Rush Street in Shock Over Death of Doctor," *Chicago Today*, March 3, 1972, p. 20.

If such was the case, I must have been doing something wrong because I didn't make a lot of money, even though I had a wad in my pocket which I intended to keep.

"A lot of money? I suppose, compared to the next best thing."

"Which is?"

"Breaking into your house and stealing your stuff."

She looked down at her cigarette again. "Hardly different from what they do anyway. They come into town, get into a club, develop a following, then cook up schemes and start ripping people off. Their days are free, so they find someone's wife to screw while the old man is at work. I think they purposely mess things up for themselves so they can leave town and start fresh somewhere else. That sound like you?"

She flipped out a switchblade and with great precision sliced the filter off her cigarette.

I said no, it did not sound like me, but it could describe some other hypnotists I'd heard about.

"I thought you'd say that. You seem more the brainy type. Someone who sits around and reads books. Thick ones. Am I right or am I wrong?"

"You could be right."

"So, what do you read?"

"Right now, it's Nabokov."

"What the hell is that? You know, if I had my choice—oh, here's Franny."

I immediately recognized her as one of the subjects from my last show, with the black hair and red lipstick under a Frida Kahlo mustache. The sleeve cuffs of her tight, beige sweater were turned back to reveal a down of dark hairs on the back of each wrist. She gave off the same humid waft of White Shoulders perfume I remembered from the stage.

"Is everything okay?" asked the ostrich, holding the filterless cigarette between her fingers like she was about to light it, but did not. Then she said to me, "She eats her hair. It's a nervous habit. She twists it around her finger and sucks on the strands until they break off and she swallows it. It gives her hairballs like a cat."

It seemed like this was one of those female friendships where one is dominant and the other submissive, a binary where one provided the personality and the other provided the looks.

Franny spoke for the first time. "It's a habit I've had since I was sixteen. I'm Catholic, or was then. After I had sex for the first time, I felt horribly guilty so I went to confession and told the priest. He asked me if I was married and I said no. He told me sex was like dope and if I wasn't careful, I'd turn into a slut. I thought, oh God, maybe I *am* a slut because sex was all I thought about. That's when I started eating my hair."

A side effect of distorting behavior for laughs is being privy to maladies such as this one. After seeing subjects cram newspaper in their clothing thinking it was uncut sheets of $100 dollar bills, a woman came to me afterward and took up an hour of my time telling me all the useless purchases she made that week as a compulsive spender. After subjects sucked laughter out of the air with a soda straw, a man approached me and asked if I could help him stop sucking his thumb. I don't know what inspired another man to tell me he had a morbid fear of sudden death while sitting on the toilet. Could hypnosis help? I did not want to hear about these conditions, but since I was a public person, I had to. They'd already gone to doctors and shrinks who were unable to help them. Some were blown off with the advice to "see a hypnotist," which a few did, but that didn't work either. They saw me as a last, desperate resort, completely ignoring the fact that I was an entertainer and not a therapist. Sure enough, Franny's friend asked me to hypnotize her to stop eating her hair.

As a hypnotic subject, Franny was not especially responsive, but I kept her on the stage because in that tight sweater she was an attractive ornament. Anything that helped my presentation was welcome. Men in the audience made it obvious they liked the way she worked her tongue during the ice cream cone eating contest, as well as her squealing attempt to cover herself with a small piece of paper when I told everyone their clothes had disappeared.

I could see how another hypnotist of the kind her friend just mentioned might be all too eager to treat this shy, over-sexed thing in a tight sweater, then treat himself to her. I had already characterized myself as not being like that, but I can't say the thought did not enter my mind. I put it aside, more or less. Maybe less. Maybe a lot less. Anyway, in this pheromone-laden atmosphere I saw myself in a position to rescue this helpless lass at who knows what benefit to myself. After all, *they* approached *me*, and this was a night club where it was no secret everyone's motives were self-serving. As a practical matter, I had one more performance that night and Franny had already proven to be hypnotizable. If she stayed on the premises, she might go up onstage again and I would be guaranteed at least one workable subject. I gave in and proceeded to hypnotize her there at the table, even though I had no experience working with a condition such as hers. People quickly noticed her slumped in her chair and a crowd of onlookers gathered. The ostrich with the unlit cigarette surveyed the situation with apparent satisfaction. I told Franny that whenever her fingers went to twirl her hair, she would become hyper-aware of doing it and consciously choose to occupy her hand with something more appropriate. That might not have been the right thing to say, but it was all I could think of. When I told her she could open her eyes, she looked around at all the people watching, at which point the little show starring her was over.

Shortly afterward Franny and friend left, so she was not in my next demonstration after all. They had gotten their parcel of attention out of me and I didn't think I'd see either of them again. But the next night they were back. Franny wore a different tight sweater, but there was something about her nose. It was red and chafed like she had a cold. Her friend took me aside and said, "She's not right. After you told her to stop eating her hair, her nose began to itch and no matter how hard she scratched, the itch wouldn't go away. Fix her!"

The times I allowed myself to be pressured into these one-off private sessions, the subjects would usually go away and I'd never hear from them again, which was fine. That's what I wanted. But once in a while they came back and I'd have to deal with why it didn't work, or worse, become obligated to further sessions in inconvenient places like this one. Even in a therapeutic setting, treating a "functional somatic syndrome" is reported to have a high failure rate, precisely why I did not want my time taken up with it. I once turned down a desperate man with one lung who said he had to quit smoking or he'd be dead in a year. He'd pay me whatever I wanted, but I did not want his or anyone else's money, however much. I suppose I could have been charitable in his case and at least given the poor soul a chance (for free), but what do I tell the woman who can't breathe even though doctors find nothing physically wrong with her? I was constantly reminded how plentiful these cases were, how they populated the world around me. I could put ants in someone's pants and make them forget their last name, but I could not help the man with something in his eye no ophthalmologist could find, or the man who lost all his hair after a vicious slur, or someone who hyperventilated whenever they saw the color yellow, or the woman whose husband could only be aroused by vinyl purses.

There were those who did not have a physical affliction, but found other ways to control me. Call it a weak moment, call it selfish intent, call it a lapse of judgement, I fell into their traps. A man who repaired gas fireplaces for a living told me he forgot where he buried a large amount of gold coins so his wife would not get them in a divorce settlement. He said he'd cut me in on a nice reward if I could hypnotize him to remember where they were. He seemed honest and likeable, and there appeared to be something in it for me, so we did a session, then went out with shovels and started digging. There were more sessions and more digging. It took a while, but finally I realized I'd been had. The American Psychiatric Association assigns a specific diagnostic category (DSM-IV-TR) to this type of compulsive lying and terms it "factitious disorder." It would describe the little pumpkin of a man who went around to bars, fitness clubs, check-out lines, anywhere he could find a captive audience—including me—with the claim he had given George Lucas the idea for *Star Wars*. Or the martial arts instructor who convinced a number of people that he was once a programmed assassin for the CIA. (This is known clinically as "pseudologia fantastica," something I can easily induce onstage: *"From now on you are a porn star!"*) He seemed to know all the jargon and coded acronyms of the spy business, but the real convincer was when he spontaneously broke into Chinese, but claimed he couldn't remember how he learned it. Someone was so impressed they contacted a local TV station and told them he should be hypnotized on the air to recover his memory of how he learned Chinese. The program director at the station smelled something funny, but sent out a crew anyway just to see what they'd get. Even though I had suspicions of my own, I saw an opportunity for publicity (*As seen on TV!*) that might lead to further engagements and sustain my supposedly lush income. Before the film crew came out, I tape recorded one of the assassin's effusions in Chinese, then went to a Chinese restaurant and played it back for the cooks in the kitchen. No one recognized it as either Cantonese or Mandarin. I went to several other Chinese and Mongolian restaurants and no one recognized the language as any dialect they knew. It was only gibberish that sounded like Chinese, a phenomenon known in psychiatry as "Wernicke's aphasia," also something I can induce onstage, as when I get subjects to speak—and translate—the Martian language. I passed this information on to the TV station, which confirmed their suspicion all along that it was a hoax. I did not mention this to the assassin, but I did mention it to several people in his circle. They didn't care. They were still convinced and continued to give him the attention he sought.

I don't know what category Franny represented since factitious symptoms are reported to be "fluid across affective and somatic boundaries." Whatever the case, I could not walk away from it any more than she could. I had to fix her. I was like my cousin who found himself in that third-floor room. With a mind highly trained in differential diagnosis he was capable of questioning why he should go up there, but he did not. For all of my experience in manipulation, I let it happen to me.

I hypnotized her again at their table, and once more a crowd of onlookers gathered. This time I told her that whenever she felt her nose itch, she would hum a low tone. It was all I could come up with. Once the brief session was over, she opened her eyes and looked around at all the people watching. Her long-necked friend did the same. They seemed pleased to have gotten everyone's attention again, including mine. On my next performance Franny went up as a subject again, for which I was grateful because I didn't have much to work with otherwise. I hoped to get some mileage out of her tongue licking the imaginary ice cream cone, but things never got that far. From the start I heard her making a low, persistent hum that became a distraction to the other subjects, so I held the mic aside and from behind leaned over with my lips to her perfumed ear (as physically close as I would ever get) and said, "You're now wide awake. Please leave the stage."

She opened her eyes and looked at me confused. She did not leave. This upset my timing with the other subjects who were marginal to begin with and my entire performance now hung on the verge of falling apart. She was a threat to my show, my livelihood, my *ego*, so I made a gesture—perhaps a bit impatient—for her to get the hell off the stage *now*.

Upon finishing my less than successful demonstration, Franny's friend urgently intercepted me.

"Franny's crying. She thinks she did something wrong. You haven't fixed her!"

Under their continuing control, I conducted another session at their table while a crowd watched. That's when I noticed something I'd seen previously but did not regard as important. The night before, onstage, her eyes opened just for an instant, hardly more than a blink. That was not uncommon among subjects and differed from someone who opens their eyes for a longer peek, which indicates they're not under. A transitory blink from the stage is not noticeable to the audience and so does not challenge my credibility. I usually let it pass. In this case, at their table, the eye-peek was close enough that someone saw it and said, "She opened her eyes. I think she's faking." The peek seemed to be for the purpose of seeing how much attention she was getting. I noticed her friend also survey the surrounding crowd. I said that on the count of three she would open her eyes, and all my suggestions—*on and off stage*—would be cleared and "everything will be back to the way it was before I showed up." If I could not cure her problem, at least I would not leave her with another one.

In a chapter contributed to *Factitious Disorders in Medical and Psychiatric Practices* (1997), Dr. Alan J. Cunnien concluded that psychosomatic syndromes such as Franny's were a way to cope with identity problems, like her self-assessment of "slut," as suggested by her priest. By eating her hair, she was eating her thoughts about herself. The bad ones. The ones she couldn't keep down. Other contributors to the same volume stated that such an affliction could exert an unusual amount of control over others. As early as 1838 observers noticed that some hypnotic subjects, mostly female, were using their responses to manipulate their hypnotists. They actually appeared to have exchanged roles and as a result were the ones who got all the attention. Who, some asked, was hypnotizing whom?[1] Franny's little routine happened to play into her own needs as well as those of her dominant friend, and together they played a game that pulled in me and who knows how many others.

When I walked out of the Follies for the last time, I saw her and her friend with a couple of young swains, one with a foot-long goatee and the other in a captain's hat. Franny was sucking away on a plug of hair in her mouth and her friend was holding forth, gesturing with a hand holding a cigarette that was still, so far as I could tell, unlit.

---

1 Alison Winter, *Mesmerized: Powers of Mind in Victorian Britain* (1998), p.78.

4 - Murder in a Chicken Suit: The Semanticist and Lana Turner's Last Husband

The Great Maurice was right when he said, "I know you're gonna steal whatever you can." I did. Others have done the same to me and I'd like to see their bodies in trash bags along the roadside. It shows how venal staged influence can be. Poets steal too, but at least with a pretense of artfulness. The youthful Robert Lowell (later awarded the Pulitzer Prize for poetry) pitched a tent on poet laureate Allen Tate's front lawn while copying and imitating his modernist style. "He is potentially a nuisance," Tate admitted, which proved correct when police had to take Lowell away from Tate's house in handcuffs. Tate himself was not above copying. He admitted rewriting one of Baudelaire's poems, stopping short of word for word plagiarism. One of his biographers described it as "aesthetic empathy rather than imitation."[1] I'm not sure if that would describe a would-be hypnotist slipping into another hypnotist's audience with a video camera, or posing as an agent asking for a demo tape, then stealing an entire act, every word, every throw-away line, joke, and facial gesture. I admit I filched the Great Maurice's Sheep in Mating Season routine and his Porno Movie Soundtrack, but modified them in a process Harold Bloom called "a swerve away from the precursor." But I'm sure The Great Maurice wouldn't have put it that way.

It's a cliché in the business that hypnotists are their own best subjects. Practicing hypnotic influence can lead to an

---

1 William Doreski, *The Years of Our Friendship, Robert Lowell and Allen Tate* (1990), p. 8, 19, 20, 43, 44, 89.

obsession for power that makes theft a mere detail. What do you call it when someone becomes so preoccupied with your power to control people in a suggestive state that they attach themselves to the essence of who you are and feed off that essence for the rest of your life? You become successful through your accomplishments and this mesmeric parasite grows along with you, so that no one can ever remember you without remembering them. Could there be, in some language, somewhere, a word for such a thing?

Dr. Michael Dean was the house hypnotist at a San Diego nightclub called the Gaslight Supper Club, appearing night after night, month after month, gathering a substantial cult following. It was the perfect deal and seemed it could go on forever. Dr. Dean always made it known that he was the world's *only* stage hypnotist to have a *legitimate* PhD. All the other "Doctors" and "Professors" that littered the trade acquired their "degrees" from diploma mills or were simply self-conferred. He was known to state most vociferously that one *must* have a doctorate from an accredited university to even *think* about making someone crow like a rooster.

Under his legal name of Sanford I. Berman, he received his doctor of philosophy degree in 1958 from Northwestern University in Chicago. His dissertation, *A Comparative Treatment of Fact, Inference and Causation in the Theory of Argumentation and of General Semantics* was based on the writings of Count Alfred Habdank Korzybski, a charismatic Polish émigré, who gained short-term popularity with his eight-hundred-page tome of obfuscation titled *Science and Sanity* (1933). Korzybski's thesis was that we should communicate more clearly, or go nuts. Example: "The multiordinality of terms is the fundamental mechanism of the full conditionality of human semantic reactions; it eliminates an unbelievable number of the old animalistic blockages, and is fundamental for sanity." That's on page 15, with 785 pages more of the same.[1]

Dean studied under semanticist and best-selling author S. I. Hayakawa, one of Korzybski's protégés. Hayakawa asserted

---

1 Buried at the end of a long footnote in Appendix V on page 281: "The term 'General Semantics' was introduced in 1933 as a technical term in an empirical natural science of evaluation which deals with living human reactions and has nothing to do with 'logic'…"

that the statement, "This is a cow" is false. You must say, "Bossie is a neuro-physico-chemical eventfulness."[1] During the height of its popularity in the 1930s and 1940s, this method of verbal correctness made impressive claims. One could be cured of homosexuality or nymphomania in as little as one hour of general semantic treatment. It could keep the fillings from falling out of your teeth.[2] In the same way that mesmerism dropped from serious notice after Mesmer was laughed out of Paris, articles on general semantics dropped from listings in the *Reader's Guide to Periodical Literature* after 1951. Nonetheless, Dean continued to be a lifelong booster.

Although he never practiced it himself, Korzybski proposed eliminating the word "is" in order to make a happier world free from wars and madness. With statements such as, "You think as much with your big toe as with your brain," he purportedly influenced the greatest minds of his generation, such as William Burroughs, who attended Korzybski's lectures in the late 1930s before the famous junkie fell for Scientology and the belief that you could store an orgasm a box. Ted Morgan points out in his biography of Burroughs that the "Ordinary Men and Women" chapter in *Naked Lunch* (1959), where "a man taught his asshole to talk," can be traced directly to Korzybski's philosophy of social engineering, perhaps shifting the importance of the big toe to another part of the body.[3] In his Preface to the 1957 edition of *Science and Sanity,* Dr. Russell Meyers, College of Medicine, State University of Iowa, declares that "the impact of Korzybski's work on Western culture is now unmistakable and there is every reason to be optimistic that his precepts will be read by ever-widening circles."[4] Korzybski's relevance to intellectual history is indicated in the eight-volume *Encyclopedia of Philosophy* (1967), where he has distinguished himself by meriting one entire sentence.

---

1 *New Republic*, Aug. 2, 1939.
2 "New Kind of Sense," *Time Magazine*, Aug. 11, 1941. Also in Korzybski's introduction to the 1948 Preface of *Science and Sanity*, "dental caries can have a semantogenic source," p. xxvi.
3 *Literary Outlaw* (1988), p. 71.
4 *Science and Sanity* (1957 edition), p. 32.

Enter Ronald Dante, stage name of the tall, gorgeously handsome Ronald Pellar. Eight years younger than Dean, he briefly attended the University of Wisconsin, then dropped out. After seeing Michael Dean's act at the Cairo Supper Club in Chicago he became so entranced by the older hypnotist that no matter where Dean performed, Dante was somewhere in the room watching Dean's act, his routine going word for word into Dr. Dante's mind. He legally changed his first name to "Doctor," thereafter calling himself "Dr. Dante," and approached the managers at venues where Dean was featured and offered to do "the same act at half the price." Dante became the itch that would not go away. When Dean went to Los Angeles, Dante followed. When he went to Hawaii, Dante went there too. *I can do the same thing for half the price.* This went on for fifteen years.

When he was not stealing Michael Dean's business at places like the Peppermint Lounge in LA, the elegantly dressed and coifed Dr. Dante rode around Hollywood on a motorcycle impressing women. One night he strode into a disco on Sunset Strip called the Candy Store and presented himself to a broken-down actress coming off her sixth messy divorce and a failed TV series. Her name was Lana Turner. Succumbing to what she called his "persuasive voice" and "strange compelling eyes," she married him on May 9th, 1969.[1]

Now with an entree to the world of celebrities, Dante began to appear in numerous photos with all the stars of the day: Bob Hope, Johnny Carson, Sammy Davis Jr., Buddy Hackett and the rock band Cream. A close examination of these photos shows some of the celebrities looking up at Dante while he smiles at the camera, giving the impression they are admiring him. Archivist Jennifer Sharpe, an expert on Dante who interviewed him for public radio, pointed out to me, given Dante's proclivity for subterfuge, that he may very well have made a funny noise or touched their buttocks just before the shutter snapped to get them to look up at him.

Dr. Dean, meanwhile, realizing there was no money in teaching young people how to think with their big toe, moved to San Diego and secured an open-ended engagement at the

---

1 *The Lady, The Legend, the Truth* (1982), p. 286.

Gaslight Supper Club, where he found bountiful emolument in staging his hypnotic buffoonery, something that did not go unnoticed by Dante. In addition to the Gaslight gig, Dean booked himself as a public speaker, instructing people on how to be happy and successful. You could purchase any of his more than one hundred and forty self-help tapes where he spoke in a strange, electronically altered voice. The box liner for *How to Gain Self-Assurance* (1974) shows him as the direct opposite of Dante, with a funny suit, sideburns, and what looks like a black poodle-poof coming out of his forehead, making him look part Elvis, part Harpo Marx. On side B he says, "Become a phony for a week and soon it will become the real you." This is what raked him in between $2,000 and $6,000 a week in 1960s dollars.

Dr. Dante, easier on the eyes, was not doing too badly himself. Even though they were legally married three years, it took him only a few months to defraud the erstwhile Hollywood beauty out of $200,000 dollars in cash, $100,000 in jewelry, and forged documents that allowed him, among other things, unlimited use of her name.[1] Waking up from Dr. Dante's influence, she got rid of him. By court order he returned some of her money before absconding to Tucson. No longer able to feed off Lana Turner, he had to go back to feeding off Michael Dean by doing Dean's stolen act at a dive appropriately called the Pirate's Den. But his imitated skills began to falter. He developed stage fright and a stuttering problem. Perhaps in desperation he listened to one of Dr. Dean's self-improvement tapes containing the profound wisdom, "if you prepare yourself, you will be able to handle anything." Dante's idea of preparing himself was to load up on tranquilizers and barbiturates, but that resulted in missing a show because he simply forgot about it.[2] Attendance at his Pirate's Den performances dwindled. He did so poorly at an engagement in Lubbock, Texas that he was charged with "theft under false pretext" and forced to return the client's money.[3]

In another gem of advice Dean stated, "Instead of waiting for someone to give you what you want, why not throw

1 Ibid.
2 *Pima Co. Arizona Case No A-25150*, Item B16.
3 Ibid.

all false excuses aside and frankly go out and get it? Courage is the indisputable weapon." If Dante was in fact listening to Dean's advice, perhaps all the tranqs and downers led him to misinterpret "indisputable weapon." On New Year's Eve, 1974, Dr. Dante met three men in a Tucson parking lot, gave them $1,420 in cash, and instructed them to go to San Diego, locate Dr. Michael Dean, and with a Colt Woodman .22 caliber pistol blow his brains out. With the dog-groomed professor out of the way, Dante planned to slip into San Diego and snatch up that lucrative, long-term engagement at the Gaslight Supper Club. With no competition, there'd be no need to work for half price.

Dante quietly removed himself to Los Angeles and popped downers while waiting for the happy news. A day passed, then another day, and finally a whole week went by and Dr. Dean was still alive. Then one sunny California morning the heavily sedated mesmerist was roused from a stupor to find himself slapped in handcuffs under a fugitive warrant for attempted murder. What could possibly have gone wrong with such a perfect plan? In applying his semantic skills to persuade someone else to do his dirty work, Dr. Dante had unwittingly hired an undercover cop.[1] He was brought back to Tucson for trial.

After a stint of detoxification and commitment to two mental wards, a court-appointed psychiatrist reported that even though Dante had "a fundamental thought disorder," he was sane enough to stand trial.[2] His $6 million lawsuit for false arrest was immediately thrown out of court.[3] When he tried the I-couldn't-remember-a-thing defense, no one believed it. After his photo appeared in the paper, the dashing Dante attracted hordes of female courtroom admirers who witnessed the jury finding him guilty of attempted murder in the 2nd degree. His motion for a new trial was denied. While out on a $5,000 surety bond put up by his brother, he skipped town, grew a beard and tried to become someone known as Lawrence Jeffers. He was recaptured in a Santa Barbara motel with forged identity papers and a bag of cash.[4] In an attempt to play on the

---

1 *LA Times*, Jan. 9, 1974, p. 3.

2 *Arizona Daily Star*, Aug. 13, 1974

3 Ibid., Aug. 3, 1974.

4 *Arizona Daily Star*, Jan. 23, 1976.

sympathies of Judge Alice Taubman at his sentencing, Dante's attorney submitted an affidavit stating he had (in the meantime) "married the mother of his only child" (a daughter). Dante's wife, identified at Elizabeth Dante of Reseda, California, appears to have been present at the sentencing.

But it was not enough to keep him out of the clink. In February of 1976 he began a 7-to-20-year term at the Arizona State Prison in Florence. Still trying to work his charm on Judge Taubman, he asked her to return the $1,400 he used to pay the undercover cop to kill Dean since "it was no longer of any evidentiary value to the State of Arizona." It worked. She ordered the money "returned to the defendant forthwith."[1] One would hope he had the decency to give it to the mother of his only child.

All this would seem to have put an end to Dr. Dante. But a few years later something happened that scarcely anyone noticed. Page 452 of the 1996 *Guinness Book of World Records* stated that the highest fee ever paid to a public speaker—over $3 million—went to someone named Dr. Ronald Dante. He spoke on—what else?—hypnotism, at a conference right in the middle of Michael Dean's old stomping grounds, Chicago.

The murder for hire story has been known among hypnotists and other entertainers for years but no one knew—or really cared—about the details. Nor did anyone know the whereabouts of the participants. By the time I started investigating Dean and Dante they would have been close to their eighties, if alive at all. In *How to Lessen Misunderstandings* (1962) Dean wrote that "stupidity is the refusal to ask questions." Since I had questions to ask, why be stupid? I decided to "throw all false excuses aside," as Dean advised, and seek some answers.

If you want to locate a magician, you start calling magicians. If you want to locate a ventriloquist, you start calling ventriloquists. But if you want to locate a hypnotist you find out very quickly how elusive they can be when it comes to any hypnotist other than themselves. I turned to Lana Turner's autobiography, *The Lady, The Legend, the Truth* (1982), where

1 *Pima Co. Arizona Case No A-25150, Fische 11, Minute Entry B2.*

she says of Dante, "his real name was Ronald Pellar, and he called himself a doctor, although of what I'm not exactly sure." Through someone I knew in the California Department of Motor Vehicles I found that there was a recent speeding citation issued to a Ronald Pellar of Huntington Beach. I got the address and wrote to Mr. Pellar asking if he was also known as Dr. Dante and would he agree to talk to me.

A week later I received a letter on the official stationery of Columbia University, with a coat of arms at the top of the page and a banner that read, "Achievement Through Education." Didn't I read in one of Dean's books that he obtained his master's degree from Columbia University? The letter read, "Thank you for your interest. I will be in touch with you shortly." It was signed, "Ron Dante."

Michael Dean stated in another one of his recordings, "a college diploma is not an all-powerful open sesame to success ... education is a state of mind, not a diploma that is earned." While Dean is known to have endowed chairs in general semantics at various colleges, Dante topped that by creating an entire university. It was not the Columbia from which Dean received his Master's Degree, but the Columbia University in Metarie, Louisiana, advertised in *Time, Newsweek, Forbes, USA Today*, and all the in-flight magazines.[1] For as little as $2,000 one could earn a PhD in a *week*. The advertisements showed an impressive building on a campus where classes were supposedly held, but the "campus" was really a mail drop at Mail Boxes Etc. Thousands of people worldwide, from politicians to TV hosts to one nuclear power plant technician in DeWitt, Illinois, got their doctorate degrees from Dante's Columbia University.[2] The FBI would later find two staffers at the Clinton White House with such degrees. Two Nobel laureates, Kenneth G. Wilson and Sune Bolgstrom (with legitimate doctorates from legitimate universities), were given honorary degrees so their names could be printed on the Columbia University letterhead. Dante's fake university

---

1 "Diploma Mills: The $200-Million-a-Year Competitor You Didn't Know You Had," John Bear, *QuackWatch*, March 10, 2002 (now a dead link).
2 *Arizona Daily Star*, Jan. 23, 1976.

reportedly made him over $75 million dollars. The Department of Justice put the figure at a mere $10 million.[1]

When I first heard Dr. Dante speak on the phone, I understood what Lana Turner meant by his soothing voice. Instead of the husky, belabored utterances of an elderly man, he spoke in a deep hypnotic tone that sounded decades younger. He was gracious and forthcoming, as if we had been friends for years, telling me he was working on wife number seven and taking up hang gliding. He went on to say he was in trouble again, this time with federal authorities over one of his other schools, Permanetics Institute, that certified people in the art of cosmetic tattooing.

"So now I'm up to eleven counts of contempt of court, which could get me twenty-two fucking years in jail. [It was actually forty-five.] I'm in Europe now, but I can't tell you where, or you could be charged as an accessory." His dispute with the Federal Trade Commission, he said, was over the semantic distinction between "permanent" and "virtually permanent." The Institute's training in cosmetic tattooing consisted of a few minutes of practice on a cantaloupe.

I had no way of knowing that he was not calling me from Europe, but from Ensenada, Mexico, where he was living on an eighty-foot $1.5 million-dollar yacht, reportedly burying suitcases of money in the desert and involved in the deaths of two people.[2]

He did not balk when I asked him about the time he tried to murder Michael Dean. Echoing the title of Lana Turner's book, he said, "there's his truth, my truth, the real truth, and the mythological truth." He was extraordinarily frank, telling me about the twenty-seven-year-old undercover snitch in Tucson named Ed Wagner, an ex-cop Dante said "liked to beat up bums so much he got kicked off the force" and, according to Dante, threatened to cut off people's fingers. To Dante he seemed to have the appropriate values necessary to snuff out an inconvenient semanticist.

"The conversations I had with Wagner were tape recorded while I was wiped out of my fucking mind on

---

1 *U.S. Department of Justice Press Release*, Los Angeles Office, April 18, 2003.
2 *Chronicle of Education*, June 25, 2004, p. A20.

prescription drugs. And they were of such poor quality no one could understand them." He said that his lawyer, whom the *Arizona Star* reported as arguing the case along meticulous lines of legal citation, was "a cocaine addict falling off his chair." The whole case, he told me, was one big conspiracy against him and that Dean had hypnotized someone to murder Dante's cousin, then paid the undercover cop $4,000 to entrap Dante.

During the course of two long phone conversations, supposedly from Europe, Dante told me his entire life story without a trace of malice, not even toward Dean, whom he said "did a good hypnosis act, even though he hasn't changed it in twenty-five years." Dante said he always seemed to marry rich women, like after World War II when he married a woman in Bangkok, whose wealthy family had him shot and left for dead. She nursed him back to health and bore him a daughter named Lee. Then there was Miss Texas and a few other unnamed lucky ones. And, of course, Lana Turner. He had a "godson" who was a hypnotist in Las Vegas, but couldn't remember his name (Bob Kensington). I asked if Dante was still performing and he said no, the last time he hypnotized anyone was in prison, where he "hypnotized the warden and his twelve-year-old daughter and treated them both for cocaine addiction."

The question I could not ask—because I didn't know of his activities in Mexico—was this: with millions of dollars and a yacht, and the means to live in luxury anywhere in the world for the rest of his life, why did he choose the grubby Mexican town of La Salina to start up a penny-ante paraglider service and hypnotize a German pilot into what one witness called "just a shell"? The answer would come, not from Dante, but from one of his intended hypnotic subjects, Brian Shook, who originally taught him paragliding and was instrumental in having Dante kidnapped off his yacht by Mexican *federales* and extradited to the US.[1]

After the police told Michael Dean he was supposed to be dead by January 6, 1974, he told the *Los Angeles Times*, "It's a complete shock to me. I haven't talked to Dante in ten or fifteen years." At the trial he made a show of sobbing into a

---

1 Private e-mail, May 17, 2003.

handkerchief and accusing Dante of causing him unspeakable misery ever since he stole his act in Chicago and followed him across the country from one nightclub to the next.[1]

I contacted the universities where Dean was supposed to have taught, but was told they did not keep records of adjunct teaching appointments, something of which Dante was perhaps aware, since he too claimed to have taught at the same universities, something that could not be proven false. I started reading Dean's *Why Do We Jump to Conclusions?* and *The Closed Mind*, both compilations of the works of others on general semantics published in 1965 under his legal name of Sanford I. Berman. The publisher of *How to Lessen Misunderstandings* was given as the International Society for General Semantics with a post office box in San Francisco. An organization with the same name had a website devoted to Korzybski's cult of "clarity." Its home page began with a one-sentence paragraph, "Alfred Korzybski, with his subject General Semantics, introduced a bunch of principles that are conducive to the whole systems view."

I called the phone number on the website, and got a recording that said, "this call cannot be completed as dialed." I wrote to their San Francisco address but the letter was returned unopened. I discovered other "General Semantics" organizations and websites, each purporting to be the correct one, like so many Deans and Dantes, Bermans and Pellars. The Institute of General Semantics (IGS) listed Sanford Berman as past president, but contacting this organization brought me no closer to speaking with Dr. Dean.

As close as I could get was locating a magician who introduced himself to Dean after seeing his hypnosis act at Iron World, a Minnesota theme park. Dean reportedly told him, "If I knew you were an entertainer, I'd have had you thrown out!" Another magician who happened to be from Dean's hometown of Virginia, Minnesota, told me that he too saw his act and introduced himself afterward. "When I told him I was a magician he went off on me like the Fourth of July. I have never to this day experienced such a bizarre encounter."

---

1 *Arizona Daily Star*, Oct. 29, 1974.

I hired a private investigator, Philip Gatewood in Milwaukee, who worked for the Catholic Church on discrediting child abuse allegations. It did not take him long to find Dean in Las Vegas. I would have called him myself but suspected he might have known I was a hypnotist and "go off on me like the Fourth of July." Besides being a detective, Gatewood was also a part-time journalist with a weekly arts column titled "The Blues Detective," so I thought that would give him a credible cover for doing an interview.

Gatewood sent me the taped phone conversation with Dean that had better audio quality than the one made of Dante planning to kill him. Although Dean described himself in *Words, Meaning and People* as "average" and "low-key," his conversation with Gatewood was antagonistic and defensive from the beginning, demanding to know how Gatewood got his number and where he was calling from. To say the conversation was difficult is an understatement. I listened to Gatewood's repeated attempts to pry something out of Dean on the murder for hire case, and each time Dean chastised him for his "incorrectness of thought." The discourse that followed could be described by the chapter titles in Dean's (Berman's) *Words, Meaning and People*: "The Problem of Communication," "Dangers Lurking in Our Assumptions," "Learning to Control Response," "Delaying Jumps to Conclusions," "Bypassing of Communication." As a detective, Gatewood was skilled at interrogation, even taught interview techniques to police departments, so he easily sparred circles around the professor of semantics. At one point Gatewood deftly shifted to complimenting Dean on being "one of the top names in twentieth century stage hypnotism," to which Dean answered "uh-huh" in agreement. Gatewood used this diversion as a chance to mention my name to see Dean's reaction. Dean said he never heard of me, but I probably stole his act. Then he mentioned Pat Collins, the female hypnotist famous in Las Vegas, and claimed she also stole his act. In fact, *every* hypnotist alive stole his act. Again, Gatewood brought up Dante's murder attempt. Dean bypassed the question by saying he was rewriting Korzybski's *Science and Sanity* and "doing research applying general semantics to the philosophy of science, Einstein's theory of relativity and quantum mechanics."

Gatewood took another tack by asking how he learned hypnotism and whether there was any truth to *Dante's* claim that he learned it in Chicago from a singing waiter with a Polish accent. Dean snapped back, "Dante's a psychopathic liar. He's sick. Don't write this, though. He's a dangerous guy."

In a roundabout way, the detective got Dean to say he became a stage hypnotist not to entertain, but "to show people that hypnosis is true," and that this initial exposure to truth-seeking was at the Cairo Supper Club in Chicago, where Dante first saw his act. He recalled the time Dante tried to assert himself on a waitress, and her boyfriend pulled a gun on him. Someone knocked it out of his hand. There was the time Dante sent a drink over to Dean as a courtesy, but Dean refused it because he knew Dante was "a psychopathic liar." That was the extent of Dean's comments on Dante.

Sanity is a theme that often comes up in general semantics, and Dean mentions it frequently in his books and tapes. With his diagnosed "thought disorder" Ronald Dante hovers over Dean's work like a mad ghost, as in the long section from the recording *How to Gain Self Assurance*, where he describes a personality he calls "the bluffer [who was] sent to prison for counterfeiting and other illegal acts." Chapter 26 in *Words, Meaning and People* is titled "Beware of Charlatans" and could just as easily be titled "Beware of Ronald Dante." During the course of the wildly evasive interview Dean mentioned that he made a two-hour audiotape on the "psychopathic personality." Under an assumed name I wrote to him at his Las Vegas address and asked if I could buy a copy of that tape, but received no reply.

In the middle of his trial on ten counts of criminal contempt stemming from his cosmetic tattoo institute, Dante fled to Mexico on his yacht. In Ensenada he bought a motorized paraglider called a trike and started up a paragliding business variously called "Royal Class," "Master of Dreams," and "Fantasy Flights." Like Columbia University, it had its own coat of arms. He recruited a band of local "flunkies" as Brian Shook called them, including a German named Peter, who was "weak in character and not very bright." He told me in an e-mail, "the last time I saw Peter, I remember walking away with a strange feeling, like I wasn't really talking to him. He had death in his eyes. I always wondered how Hitler did it until I saw that going on." Dante began advertising his "fantasy flights" to tourists.

After six weeks of flying with passengers, the inexperienced Peter, under Dr. Dante's control, went up in the trike one afternoon with a "three-hundred-and-fifty-pound tourist" and buzzed over a crowded swimming pool at a resort to drum up potential customers. "He did an aerobatic maneuver," wrote Shook, "where he dropped into a sideslip, something he'd been warned about from more experienced pilots. Dante apparently told him to do it anyway. It was good for business. [The heavy weight] in the back seat changed the center of gravity. It didn't recover from the sideslip, just splattered on the beach in front of the crowd at the pool, including this guy's brother, wife and two kids. They hit so hard their bones powdered and left a crater in the beach the size of a Volkswagen."

In the confusion, according to Shook, Dante's flunkies stole everything off the corpses—wallet, watch, sidepack—as well as everything out of Peter's house and van. Disgusted by these events and Dante's crude attempts at a cover-up, there began an effort by concerned parties to have Dante brought to justice, but Dante had reportedly befriended the governor of Baja, who interfered with Mexican authorities taking action. So they notified the American news media, which began to cover Dante's activities in Mexico. Pressured by public attention, the Mexican *federales*, in conjunction with the FBI, nabbed the hypnotist on his yacht and brought him back to the US to face a maximum of forty-five years in federal prison for mail fraud and contempt charges relating to his fake schools. He was forced to give up his $1.5 million yacht (and lose the several hundred thousand dollars supposedly hidden on it) and pay more than $143,750 in consumer redress. That left millions of dollars still allegedly buried in the Mexican desert, possibly dug up and stolen by associates. Dante was sentenced to sixty-seven months in the federal correctional facility in Taft, California for his fake schools, but was never officially implicated in the paraglider incident.

Most of the work Sanford Berman (Michael Dean) published were anthologies, and his "books" were little more than cliché-ridden pamphlets with clip art covers and sold for a dollar to what he told Gatewood was "any idiot off the street." While Ronald Peller (alias Dr. Dante) was out of the way in prison, Sanford Berman (alias Michael Dean) gave up the stage and began writing again. It's unknown how far he got rewriting Korzybski's *Science and Sanity* when he died in Las Vegas on June 16, 2015. He was survived by his wife Sandra and his daughter Michele.

Sanford I. Berman is described on Wikipedia as "a philanthropist who has given over a million dollars to various universities." The accompanying photo shows him, as his stage persona, hypnotizing subjects on a Muscular Dystrophy Telethon in 1982. Having acquired substantial wealth as a hypnotist, he invested in real estate and became a millionaire. From this largesse he endowed grants for the Sanford I. Berman Debate Forum at the University of Nevada, Las Vegas; the Sanford I. Berman Chair in General Semantics at the University of California, San Diego; and the Sanford I. Berman Chair in Language and Communication at the same university. In Virginia, Minnesota he established the Sanford I. Berman Social Hall, a kind of church basement with archival photos of the B'nai Abraham Synagogue and early Jewish businesses in the region. His obit in the Virginia, Minnesota *Virginian* is titled, "Brilliant Man, Impressive Hair." The accompanying photo shows a pudgy man of advanced years in a tuxedo and jet-black hair cut in a style one might see on a fancy breed at the National Kennel Club. His arms extend to each side in an open-armed gesture of trust, the same pose struck by Dante on a publicity brochure from the days he hired the hit man. At last Dr. Michael Dean was out of the way, but too late for it be of much use to his rival.

Dante was released from prison for the second time after serving two-and-a-half years. He was seventy-six years old. All his ill-got millions disappeared, he said, in the hands of trusted business partners. He moved to a trailer park in San Diego where he lived on six-hundred dollars a month from

Social Security. He tried to start up his hypnosis show again and in keeping with the times advertised himself on Craigslist. He created a website with publicity photos of himself forty years out of date. None of it brought the former millionaire out of poverty. Changing tactics, he ran an ad in a magician's magazine offering seminars for $1,500, showing how to earn $10,000 a night doing magic shows. When that scheme failed, he attached himself to Gil Boyne, a collaborator with Ormond McGill in writing the second edition of *Professional Stage Hypnotism* (1977). Boyne operated a certification school of his own, the Hypnotism Training Institute in Glendale, California, offering PhDs in hypnotism. When I interviewed Boyne by phone, he told me that "a stage hypnotist could make a million dollars a year." When I did a few quick mental calculations on the number of available booking dates in a year and mentioned how outlandish the remuneration would have to be per show, he backtracked and said, "Some of these claims, of course, may be exaggerated." Dante followed Boyne from town to town on his seminar tours like he used to follow Dean, but Boyne was not about to share power or profit with an indigent ex-con with no reputation for honesty.[1] When Dante could no longer afford to follow Boyne's traveling lectures, he went back to his trailer and eked out a living selling artificial flowers made out of toilet paper.[2]

In 2005 I received an e-mail from his daughter Sage, who apparently knew I was researching her father. She wrote, "Supposedly he had a relationship in the late 60s with the heiress in Bangkok and had a daughter with her. I will never know for sure. When incarcerated in Arizona State in 1976, my sister was two. My mother told me stories of them going to visit and my sister would comb his hair for him with a set of keys. Yes, he has been quite an adventure. He is not doing too well with his health now, but he's just as clever as always. Thankfully he is out of jail, we're hoping for good. He doesn't have all that much time left to spend as a grandpa."

---

1 David Simone, private e-mail March 27, 2005.
2 *SignOnSanDiego.com*, Aug. 7, 2006.

5 - Can You Hear Me Back There?
Influence and the Amplified Voice

Chichi sat on my chest in a hotel in Caborca, Mexico while I projected my voice as loudly as possible, "*Su nariz es hecha de goma!*" (Your nose is made of rubber!). Suzi and Consuela heard the noise and came in our room where they fell all over each other laughing. Even though what we were doing was my idea, it was not all that original. The Emperor Nero exercised his diaphragm the same way, speaking in a prone position with sheets of lead on his chest so his voice, and influence, would carry further.

Loud is synonymous with power—as in "I profess with the *loudest voice* the truth of..." or "Capitol Hill's *loudest voice* for the bombing of..." Multiple 10,000-watt amplifiers stack up at music concerts like gun turrets in front of crowds begging for the big blow-down. When rock bands increased the volume calibrations on their equipment from the standard 10 (highest) to 11, the Marshall JCM900 amplifier appeared with a knob reading of 20 for "pure overdriven outrage on maximum."[1] Numerous groups have claimed to be the "loudest band in the world"[2] out of sheer acoustical defiance. The ear-destruction band known as Manowar manifested itself by aggressively blasting out 130 pain-inducing decibels, equal to cocking your head close to the tail of a fighter jet taking off with full afterburner thrust. Continuous sound as we know it ceases to exist at around 194 decibels,[3] and is replaced by what is perceived as a series of explosions—the nuclear kind, perhaps,

---

1 *Marshall JCM Handbook*. The threshold of pain for the human ear is 130 dB, a level reportedly marked as "infinity" on some volume control knobs.
2 en.wikipedia.org/wiki/Loudest_band
3 Wayne Staab, "An Upper Limit to Sound?" (2016) hearinghealthmatters.org

representing the ultimate merge of power and volume. With that you could make a fool not only out of anyone, but *everyone*. You could say with the ultimate in dressing room hubris, *I killed em, I slayed em, I knocked em dead!* Stage hypnotism is a similar realm of power, and volume proclaims it.

As I worked night clubs in Texas booked through an agency in Dallas, I became ever more addicted to amplification as a way to drown out background noise and heckling. I used the band's sound system, "chewing" the mic, as they say, sometimes feeling my mouth slide over the head smeared with lipstick from the female singer before me who did the same thing. To override the blender at the bar, the clack of billiard balls, jeering, forced belching, scuffles and breaking glass, I told the sound guys, "Push the treble and pull the bass. Give me all the volume you can without feedback." I wanted my voice to carry to all four walls, the parking lot, all the way to *Mexico* as I tried with everything I had to manipulate unsuspecting subjects into doing what they "wouldn't ordinarily do." It had to work, because failure was too painful. I was successful just enough times to experience a gambler's reward, thinking I was ahead whether that was the case or not. I began to notice that Mexicans were nearly always the most responsive to my efforts, both as subjects and spectators. It was like I was performing for them and everyone else was in the way. We were fans of each other.

Trance is the trickster of awareness. It connives itself upon us. We never know the exact moment it takes over any more than we know the exact moment we fall asleep. The entrancement that led to Chichi sitting on my chest began at some indeterminate point up to the time I entered the office of Jose Gutierrez in Houston. I'd heard that he was a former trapeze artist who practiced self-hypnosis to focus his concentration, but apparently it didn't work the night in San Antonio when he missed his grip and fell. Although he was caught by a safety net, he sustained some injuries that made it no longer possible for him to work on the trapeze. He briefly tried his hand at stage hypnotism, but chance did not favor him there either, so he switched to brokering obsolete thrill rides that could no longer pass inspection in the US, exporting them to carnivals in Mexico and Central America. He was a youthful fifty, or thereabouts, with salt-and-pepper hair combed straight back from a low forehead. When he stood, he came up to the level of my chin. His posture leaned slightly to one side like a floor lamp with a faulty base, a result, I assumed, of his trapeze accident. I remarked on his silver-heeled cowboy boots (which boosted his height by a couple of inches) and he commented on the big zircon I wore on my pinkie, boosting my ego by a couple of deceptive notches. As Kipling described the meeting of power with power, "There is neither border, nor breed nor birth / When two strong men stand face to face 'tho they come from the ends of the earth."

I think he was hoping I was there to cut him a check for a used Tilt O'Whirl, but his expression froze into an ellipsis when I told him—very slowly so I wouldn't have to repeat—what I did for a living. "I understand you used to do the same thing."

"It was a long time ago. Who told you that?"

I named a club manager in Galveston.

"Him? Really? I thought he was still in jail for arson. Forgive me, I'm a little confused. What would you like from me?"

"I thought you might know someone who could help me fill in some dates in Mexico."

"Mexico? Did you say Mexico?"

"No one's a prophet in their own land."

He was on the verge of smiling. "Prophet? In Mexico? I'm not understanding. *Hablas español?*"

"*Un poco.*"

He said something further in Spanish, but spoke so fast I didn't understand any of it. Nonetheless, I said, "*Voy a demonstrar a ustedes los poderes fastistico del hipnotismo.*" (I am going to demonstrate to you the strange powers of hypnotism.)

He went from almost smiling to definitely laughing. "How did you ever learn *that*?"

"I knew a cocktail waitress who once lived in Guadalajara. I had her translate key phrases into a tape recorder and then I memorized what she said."

He threw his head back and laughed uncontrollably. Finally, he composed himself and said, "To be honest with you, I only handle carnival rides. Sorry."

I gave him an intense hypnotic stare and said in a soothing voice, *"Fijen toda su atencion hacia mi!"* (Focus your attention directly on me!)

"What?" It lost its effect by having to repeat it. After another bout of laughing, he looked at me as if I were a curious-looking bug that flew in and landed on the wall.

Hypnotists have always been typecast as foreigners. Doyle's Madame Penclosa was from Trinidad; Svengali was a Jew from Germany (his deadly photo taken in "the mysterious East"); Balzac's Centenarian was born centuries earlier and lived in China, India and the New World (he's not even present where he is, but moves about in a "disembodied manner"). Count Fosco in Wilkie Collins's *Woman in White* (1860) was a traveling magician from a foreign country, and Holgrave, the mesmerist in *House of the Seven Gables,* breezed in from nowhere. The non-fictional Anton Mesmer arrived in Paris from Austria in 1778 with a serious language problem and George Baldwin brought his mesmeric mojo to Egypt in 1790. Abbé José-Custodio de Faria imported himself into France from India and Jules du Potet de Sennevoy emigrated to Britain from France, while Charles Lafontaine went from France to Italy.[1] Ben Vandermeide, "Europe's Fastest Hypnotist," moved from Rotterdam to Salt Lake City and hit the big time at state fairs and jubilees in the 1960s precisely because of his foreignness. Similarly, John Kolisch came to America from Mesmer's native land, bringing Strange Energy to college campuses from the other side of the language barrier. So the road I was trying to be on had already been well-paved for generations before me, and I told Gutierrez as much.

"Actors and entertainers," I said, "memorize lines phonetically all the time. Of course, I would need a translator onstage to help me. Ever hear of Tony Camo? He's a Mexican hypnotist who sometimes works in the US. Really good too. I heard he used an English translator at first."

He made an effort to shake off his amusement over me. Then it was time to do something about the bug. He told me again, "I only handle carnival rides. Sorry."

---

1 Alan Gauld, *History of Hypnotism* (1992).

I got up and left him the phone number of the answering machine at my mother's apartment in Milwaukee just in case. On my way out he asked if my ring was a real diamond.

"Can't you tell?"

He laughed and continued laughing as the door closed behind me.

I checked my messages by remote late at night (this was before voice mail) when the rates were cheapest, and relayed calls to and from theatrical agencies that continued booking me in cowboy dives. Time went by and I had almost forgotten about Gutierrez when I picked up a message from him asking if I wanted to work in a carnival somewhere in Jalisco. I called him back and he mentioned a "Club Macabre," but he was vague on the details. It sounded like a funhouse, but I couldn't understand what I was supposed to do. There might have been some opportunity there, but I turned him down anyway and didn't expect to hear from him again. I gave up on the Mexican pipe dream.

But then a few weeks later I got another message from him. This time he said his brother in Guaymas knew of a traveling "musical revue" looking for "something different." He was less evasive than before but, typical of agents, not a fountain of details either. Maybe, just maybe, my suggestion—*Fijen toda su atencion hacia mi!*—had worked on him without either of us knowing. He didn't mention money or commission or whether he was doing this as a favor or what, but I didn't care. The pipe dream was back.

Prophet in a foreign land... First, I had to *get* to the foreign land. Then, and only then, could I exert my imagined influence and seize the power I found so irresistible. I didn't like working without a performance agreement because night clubs had proven to be slippery operations and when pay day arrived there could suddenly arise all manner of discrepancies not in my favor. I was in no position to dictate terms, so in this case I made an exception. All Gutierrez gave me was a date and a time to be at a place called El Cache del Cid in the border town of Agua Prieta, Mexico. I was supposed to ask for someone named Humberto Ramos.

Driving through the Sonoran flatlands gave me plenty of time to imagine my new future. I stored my car at a gas station in Douglas, Arizona and crossed into Mexico where I found El Cache del Cid at the edge of town on a dark street near some railroad tracks. It was January and potholes were covered with sheets of ice. Inside it was cold and empty except for an old man in a woman's hat wiping down tables. To the side of a dance floor stood a rusted tree of spotlights and an obsolete cardioid stick mic clamped to a mic stand. On one table was a notice slightly bigger than a post card that read, *Humberto Ramos Autentico Travesti Show*. That must have been the musical revue Gutierrez was talking about. I imagined music, costumes, dancing and myself as the "something different." I held the card and saw my breath in front of me as I asked the old man, "*Esta noche?*"

He shrugged his shoulders like he didn't understand, or didn't want to be bothered.

I was supposed to meet Humberto at six, but he was not there by six-thirty or seven, or even eight. By then the old man was gone and a young bartender with a long shock of hair hanging over his face was arranging bottles and glasses behind the counter. I asked him where I could find Humberto Ramos.

"*Mas tarde,*" he said with indifference.

A few loud *hombres* gathered at the bar around a bottle of tequila and between shots they rolled dice and pushed each other in rough play that bordered on real aggression. One of them grabbed the hair-draped bartender by the shirt and yanked him half way over the counter. "*Que?*" was all he said before they let him go. He went back to arranging his glassware and they went back to playing dice and shoving each other around.

Something was apparently scheduled for nine o'clock, but by that time only a few people had gathered, mostly women. It was still cold so no one took off their coats. Finally, a female figure big as an ox, with a proportionate cleavage exposed to the frigid air, made a grand entrance through the front door with a retinue of three young men in heavy makeup carrying bundles of wardrobe. She recognized who I was immediately and, as everyone watched, pressed her hundred kilos of hot flesh right up against my body and gave me a hug, introducing herself as Maria. With steam rising from big crimson lips she said, "you like girls, hey bad boy? Real *chicas*, have real *chicas* tonight, everything you want, bad boy, you dream beeg thees time, no?"

"*Travesti*" was not in my pocket Spanish-English dictionary, but I should have been able to figure it out. This crimson-lipped mountain of garish ladyhood was actually Humberto Ramos.

I waited for some kind of discussion as to how things were supposed to go and what I was supposed to do, but everything rushed toward showtime. As close as we got was Maria telling me, "We do goo show, beeg boy, we do goo show!" Then she flipped on the stage lights and walked out on the floor. She did not use the microphone because her voice had such force that it easily carried to the back of the room. She told a series of jokes in Spanish, cupping her big bust and gesturing to the area between her legs, which brought considerable laughter from the small audience, some of whom seemed to be her friends. I heard the word "*hipnotizador,*" which caused a minor stir. In a clumsy way, "Somewhere Over the Rainbow" came on over the speaker and then went off. After a pause it came on again and out skipped Suzi (as she was introduced) in a braided Dorothy wig and blue dress with lace trim petticoat. She took the mic and lip-synced the song with the same girlish innocence as Judy Garland in *Wizard of Oz* and finished with a cute curtsey. Then Maria introduced flirtatious Chichi in gold lace-up heels and a smoky-black formal dress with netted sleeves. She did a camped-up version of "Besame Mucho." When that was over Maria told more jokes, then introduced Consuela in a black leather miniskirt and knee-high boots with spiked heels. She did "These Boots Are Made For Walkin," which made a big impression. Suzi came out again in a clinging dress of platinum sequins and a mauve boa and did "Hey Big Spender" while moving through the audience with the microphone. She sat on men's laps and tousled their hair, rousing up cackling laughter because everyone knew this sultry vamp was not really a woman. Maria came out again, detached the mic and started her version of "Piece of My Heart" by Janis Joplin, wildly tossing around her thick mane of hair. At the end of her number, she started using the word *hipnotizador* again, followed by more laughs. She made a gesture toward me indicating it was my turn. I walked out and stood at the mic, expecting it to be live, but as I started my memorized patter in Spanish I realized it was dead. I turned to Maria and tapped the mic, but all she did was look at me and smile. It was merely a prop for lip-syncing.

Having a working microphone was always an assumption. My vocal cords were adapted to the nuances of amplification which allowed for all sorts of subtle variations in tone necessary for fixing attention, as well as overpowering distractions. But now I had no choice but to continue with voice alone. My words carried only a short ways in front of me, then dropped to the floor.

At this point I began to feel I was not in a show at all, but caught up in an awkward incident. With my strained voice, and some fumbling assistance from Maria, I managed to get a few people to sit in chairs and face the audience. I said in Spanish what I knew how to say, but no one seemed to understand. In the confusion my pronunciation must have been off, evidently way off. Maria, whose English was hardly better than my Spanish, did some "translating," but that didn't help. It all went over as one big travesty. But maybe that was the point. The performers were not really women, they weren't really singing, I was in a Mexican revue without knowing Spanish, and trying to be a *hypnotizador* without hypnotizing anyone. It was the "something different," a travesty within a travesty.

The *Humberto Ramos Autentico Travesti Show* was cleverly held together on salvaged parts like the old station wagon that hauled it around. With battered equipment and costumes smelling of sweat and perfume, we chugged our way to the next town and checked into an ultra-low budget hotel with the distinct odor of smoke and char. When we went up to our rooms it became obvious that one side of it had burned away in a fire. The sleeping arrangement came down to me, Humberto and Chichi (who was apparently not gay) in one room and the other two in another. We remained at the burnt ruins a few days while Humberto (out of drag) scouted ahead to set up another engagement.

Lack of amenities did not interfere with the high level of frolic among my travel mates. They were curious about me and asked many questions, most of which I barely understood and was hardly able to answer in Spanish. Was I married? Did I have kids? Was I gay? Was I Catholic? They had a private repertoire of gestures and expressions that eventually included me and I became part of their frolic. Suzi liked to rub her shoulder up against me and say, "I lub you berry moch!" (I love you very much!), the only words she knew in English. After that all it took was a roll of either of our shoulders to get us both laughing. Consuela set little eye traps to catch me checking out her body as I tried to reconcile her with the male gender. For his part, Chichi pursued *señoritas* (or even *señoras*) with his feminine manner combined with a low voice soothing as a saxophone. Women seemed to be fascinated by this mysterious combination of polarities. I don't know how much of it led to anything, but whenever I saw him in female company, he seemed to have them quite charmed.

We finally left for another town and another cantina where again Humberto's show attracted mostly women in pairs or groups. The show was not meant for a gay audience, but it had its elusive levels of fandom. At that time in small-town Mexico, women were generally segregated from bars, but this was an exception and their chance to enjoy an evening's entertainment in a non-threatening environment. They saw it not so much as a drag show as an illusion show, something presented as one thing but was actually something else, a cultural spectacle of mystery like dashboard tableaux on velvet mats in buses and taxis, or ten-person parades with banners and costumes headed down deserted country roads. If Humberto were to try his travesty show in small town America, it would not be regarded as a flashy mirage but as something degenerate and perverted. Not that the *travestis* didn't experience the occasional voice sneering *"puto"* from a doorway, or a taunt hurled from a car, but if things got too overt Maria stepped in with her heavyweight presence and played the harassers like stooges until all they could do was go away grumbling.

Then there was the dust. I felt it on my teeth and inside my ears. It found its way into my pockets and covered the worn peso notes in my wallet. It gathered along my neckline where I developed an itchy rash. I took Chichi's advice to see a *curandero* and get something in a colorful bottle to treat it, but nothing worked. As we continued into the interior on this poorly organized tour, the "kloobs" as they called them (clubs) became little more than four walls around a bunch of people and a stack of Tecate cases. To run the lights and music they often had to snake lengths of extension cord to a power outlet far outside the building. I saw pesos exchanged at the door, but profit in all this didn't seem to come down to more than a smudge.

I had to resign myself to being the gringo foil for Maria's jokes, but as time went on, we found a coordination between us that reached a critical point when—behold a wonder!—people actually started dropping to the floor in a hypnotic trance. The first time it happened there was gasping and fearful murmuring. Spectators jumped to their feet for a better look and didn't know whether to be amused or terrified, and that included Maria herself. It put me in a whole new light. Instead of being a mere laugh in a *travesti show*, I became an overwhelming feature that relied on Maria doing the translating in her powerful voice. She realized she could embellish the translations and began making up suggestions of her own and taking over my act. It became a matter of who was the *hipnotizador*, me or her?

Humberto's *travestis* asked me even more questions I could barely understand, much less answer in Spanish. How do you do that? Is it dangerous? Can you make someone turn gay? Can you talk to ghosts? What about the Devil? There were whispers of Santería and black magic.

If you practice touching your toes with enough frequency you can get lower and lower until you are able to put your palms flat on the floor. If you practice holding your breath you can stay under water longer and longer. If you practice lifting weights, you can lift more. It's part of the body's adaptability. Why should the voice be any different? I went on a desperate campaign of improvement. To exercise what has been called "expression of the articulators," I opened my mouth and extended my tongue out as far as possible. I did not have much privacy so when Chichi saw me doing this he asked if I was okay. I stretched my lips around the rim of a plastic cup and did knee bends while reciting *concentrar... cierren los ojos* (concentrate...close your eyes...). Chichi thought there might be something wrong with me. I tried to explain, but Maria was scouting ahead for the next venue, so without her to translate, I had to make do with my limited Spanish. *"Mi voz... fuerte..."* [My voice...strong...], I said, hoping he would figure it out. With the same necessity that drove Demosthenes to fill his mouth with rocks and run up hills reciting speeches, I growled, trilled and bellowed while running in place. It wasn't long before all the *travestis* together thought I was *loco*. Centuries earlier Plutarch advised orators to do exactly what I was doing, exercise their voices, *even in public lodgings*, and ignore those who might laugh at them[1].

The *Humberto Ramos Autentico Travesti Show* made its unlikely influence without the use of an amp with a volume reading of 20. Like the barely held-together spectacle that it was, sooner or later the weakest part would fail. It did, outside Durango, when the station wagon with its loud muffler died. The show went dark. To that point I had not gotten a single peso in payment. They needed money for repairs and looked to me to provide it, which I could have done, but did not. That's when I awoke from my fantasy of casting my voice in a foreign land. It takes more than a mouth to make a prophet. It takes a mouth that can be heard. I quietly left Mexico by bus with nothing more than an itchy neck.

Long after the Mexican job, I was traveling in Greece and decided to test my voice at the outdoor Theater of Dionysus in Athens, where actors in antiquity addressed as many as 17,000 spectators, some as far away as 135 feet.[2] It was off-season in the middle of the afternoon, and since no one was around I did a quick sound check. *"Testing... hello... hello... one, two, three...*

---

1 Maud W. Gleason, *Making Men: Sophists and Self-Presentation in Ancient Rome* (1995), p. 92.

2 The width of the audience (*cavea*) was 82 meters (thehistoryhub.com/theater-of-diony-sus-facts=pictures.htm) and the depth was about half that based on photographs. An actor would have to project their voice a minimum of 135 feet to the farthest seat over 100 rows back. (engramma.it/eOS/resources/images/170/2-1%20Boletis.pdf).

focus your attention directly on me..." Even though I thought I'd trained my voice significantly in Mexico, here the words blew away in the wind before they reached the first row.

I wrote to Dr. Ingo R. Titze, author of *Principles of Voice Production* (1994), and asked him just how *loud* a human voice could possibly be. He replied that "the voice is very inefficient, so the radiated power from the mouth is a small fraction of the raw power, usually 1–10 milli-watts. Nobody has ever reported as much as 0.1 watt, but it may be possible."[1] If that were the case, I don't know how it could happen that Maria was able to fill the noisiest cantinas with no more given acoustical power than I had. It meant that millennia before the microphone, human history itself and its momentous pronouncements of faith, upheavals of thought, great axial shifts, movement of armies and consolidation of realms, all happened on no more than one tenth of a watt.

It's a seldom-pondered riddle how someone like Demosthenes, with the same wattage as everyone else (and probably less, since he was known to have a naturally weak voice), was able to speak in sentences long enough to cover one side of a sheet of papyrus and be heard at the Athenian Assembly by upwards of *six thousand* people.[2] An answer was attempted by actual experiment at the outdoor Lost Colony Theater in North Carolina that produced plays with actors instructed to use their natural voices as in antiquity.[3] Their first discovery was that temperature, wind, humidity and the rustling of trees were factors they had to consider. They tested the oft-stated hypothesis that the mouth on a stage mask was formed in such a way as to act as a megaphone to project the actor's voice (which would not, however, explain Demosthenes). Actual testing showed that far from acting as a megaphone, the mask only amplified the voice *inside* the mask with feedback the actors struggled to overcome. Eventually, they had to cheat with hidden body mics. But the ancients had

---

1 Personal correspondence 2007. Also see Chap. 3 of his *Principles of Voice Production* (2000).

2 Lionel Pearson, *The Art of Demosthenes* (1976), p. 170. And en.wikipedia.org/wiki/ Ecclesia_(ancient_Greece)

3 Rocco Dal Vera, ed., *The Voice in Violence, Essays on Voice and Speech* (2001).

their own cheats. They used professional heralds to relay words to the back rows of large crowds as well as relying on the distribution of written texts.[1] How often this happened is difficult to tell and it doesn't seem to explain everything. My oratorial mastery of Mexican cantinas was nothing compared to what Shakespeare's actors were up against in the Globe Theater, where audiences numbering in the thousands heard monologues and soliloquies of the highest refinement in the actors' natural voices. Abraham Lincoln delivered his Gettysburg Address to fifteen thousand people using nothing but the wind that came out of his body.[2] Charles Dickens did a series of readings to 2,500 people at St. James Hall in London;[3] Oscar Wilde spoke to a "standing room only" crowd of more than 1,200 at Chickering Hall in New York;[4] and in a photograph of Grover Cleveland at his Inaugural Address in 1885 he stands before what he called a "vast assemblage of my countrymen," surely in the thousands, looking very strange at a podium without a microphone.[5] In each case there are no known reports of anyone shouting, "Can't hear!" When I listen to recordings of the earliest radio broadcasts, I detect a whole glossary of speech embellishments left over from the pre-amplification era, no doubt used as an essential aid to hearing. Those embellishments have become extinct except for the remnants of lilts and drawn-out syllables that remain in the declamations of poets and preachers.

Demosthenes, Abe Lincoln, Oscar Wilde and all the rest had their day, but the age of amplification has taken over. In Mexico I found I could control my unamplified voice only to a degree. So I went on to consider other ways to increase my ear-reach—by controlling circumstances. First, there would be no more blind acceptances. No easy trust. With words chosen as carefully as those in a poem, I specified stage requirements in my contracts. At after-dinner performances, if I came on after a

---

1 *The Crowd in Rome in the Late Republic*, cited above, p. 223.
2 "Seven Score and 10 Years Ago: The Gettysburg Address," Barbara Maranzani (2018), history.com/news/seven-score-and-10-years-ago-the-gettysburg-address
3 thecircumlocutionoffice.com
4 *New York Times*, Jan. 10, 1882, p. 5, and Robert Davis, Theater Consulting Services (robertdavisinc.com).
5 pagebypagebooks.com and *Niday Picture Library*.

89

speech or awards ceremony, I insisted there not be a break before my presentation because people would trickle back in during my induction and cause a distraction. Or worse, they would take the opportunity to sneak away and go home, reducing the audience size and therefore the probability of finding workable subjects. I insisted my performing area not be at the long end of a rectangular room, because people in back would be too far away and thus tempted to start up distracting conversations. No open dance floor or buffet tables in front of the stage to obscure my visibility. If track lights above the performing area in banquet rooms were turned the wrong way (as they invariably were, usually with half the bulbs burned out), I insisted they be adjusted to shine on me and not some place to the side. This involved locating a custodian and a ladder, something that could require no small degree of assertion on my part.

But first, foremost, and absolutely, there had to be a *microphone*. As I learned in Mexico, using one provided for me is like an arranged marriage. Unfamiliar mics, if they work at all, can very likely have shorts, pops, and tinny-sounding amplification like the speakers in airplanes. If it's a wired mic, there could be an electrical short somewhere in the cord, usually just below the base of the mic, so the sound will cut out at unexpected times. No one ever thinks to fix it. They simply pass the problem on to the next speaker. Wireless mics have their own dysfunctions. No one keeps track of when the batteries were last changed, so they could go dead at any time. Signal reception is also unpredictable, with dead spots on the stage where sound cuts out, or the frequency of another wireless mic in another banquet room replacing my voice with someone else's speech or song or stupid joke.

To preempt all those problems in advance, I provide my own top-of-the-line Beta 87A wireless microphone with automatic receiver selection set to a predefined optimum frequency to avoid signal interference. The mic is connected with a balanced input jack to a Liberty Xtreme 5500 amplifier to project my voice up to 123 decibels in a narrow aim zone. To guarantee *absolutely* that nothing interferes with me being heard, I have gone to the expense of having backups to all components.

But there are still risks. After my performance, a committee person may ask on the spur of the moment, "can I use your mic to make one quick announcement?" and reach out in full expectation of me handing it over. Not so fast. It's like a stranger asking to take your baby. They hold it awkwardly too far from their lips so people shout "can't hear!" or stand in front of the amp and cause ear-splitting feedback with no idea of what to do. But I have to be a sport and hand it over anyway, always nervous they will fumble and drop it while trying to manage the fishbowl for drawing a door prize. I have to monitor them closely so they don't set it down on a table where it can roll off and hit the floor. Once damaged, a wireless mic is never the same again and they are expensive to replace.

Plutarch pointed out that nature has given us two ears and one tongue because we ought to listen more than talk.[1] Through the centuries when words publicly spoken were scarce, they may have taken on more value. People *wanted* to hear, therefore they actually heard. Hearing was less passive and more goal-directed. Where there is no glut of sound, less is more. Today an estimated 104 million people are at risk of hearing loss from *too much* sound reaching their ears, according to an article in *Environmental Health Perspectives*.[2] Amplification has given us the phrase "tune out."

History is still happening, but at many orders of magnitude louder than a tenth of a watt.

---

1 Plutarch, *Morales* (100 AD), section 3, "On Listening to Lectures."
2 Quoted by David Owen in *New Yorker* (May 6, 2019), "Is Noise Pollution the Next Big Public-Health Crisis?"

III - Culture

6 - Death by Projected Thought

After my exhibition of artificial insanity before a crowd, someone will inevitably stagger up to me with a fresh drink and wide snicker to ask (as if they were the first), "Could you ever use this, like, to *kill* someone?" Ha and ha.

Powerful influence can be dangerous influence. It's locked in a Manichaean struggle with resistance. From myth to pop lyrics, influence drives the narrative, with resistance constantly throwing itself in the way. Persuaded by a devious snake, Eve resisted God's almighty influence. Brutus blocked Caesar's dominance with a dagger to the ribs. Elvis sang about the power of his shoes (the blue suede ones) with that little problem of those who want to step on them.

After Mesmer brought his bucket of push into the world, it took on a life of its own with endless unintended consequences. The push was called "vital fluid," an invisible something that flowed through the ether between bodies and souls. By the early 1800s hypnotic subjects were often described as "cold as death itself," as if their lives hung in the balance. Spirit mediums took it further and hypnotized themselves to be the oracles speaking with, or for, others who were already dead. Shortly after Mesmer himself was no longer alive, a well-known German medium predicted in a trance the death in April, 1816 of a high-ranking person identified in *Blackwood's Magazine* only as "S. M."[1] When S. M. continued to live, a second medium moved the date to October. The effect of all this publicity on S. M., whoever that was, can only be guessed. In a subsequent report it was said "those who are

---

1 *Blackwood's Edinburgh Magazine* (1817), p. 37.

acquainted with the event do not require to be told...Many bets were won and lost."

In a century where medical knowledge could not yet determine with certainty when death had actually occurred, premature burial was not unheard of, evidenced by scratch marks later discovered inside buried coffins. Sometimes bells were rigged from inside to above ground in case the corpse should come alive. Because of this uncertainty there arose a macabre interest in mesmerism as applied to death's event horizon. In 1817, a Mrs. Zimmerman in Bielefeld, Germany was dying of tuberculosis. Her husband kept her in a mesmerized state for twenty-four days. "Life and death," it was reported, "struggled together." Whenever her husband left the room, she appeared to pass away. When he returned, she revived. Finally, he saw no way to save his wife so he left the room and let her die naturally.[1]

Ten years later a French physician named Foissac was effectively treating an epileptic patient with mesmeric suggestion to control his seizures. The doctor was surprised when the patient began to predict when his seizures would happen. Thomas de Quincey (himself under the powerful influence of opium) took an interest in the case when Foissac's patient made the shocking prediction that someday he would murder his own family. Before that tragic event could come to pass, the epileptic died in a precognitive blind spot when the mesmerist's horse ran him over with a buggy.[2]

Honoré de Balzac, who personally knew many of the leading mesmerists of his day, made hypno-death a theme in *The Centenarian* (1822), where a centuries-old serial killer uses hypnotic influence to immobilize his female victims. Tullius, the protagonist, arrives at the Centenarian's house just in time to see the killer carrying a hypnotized Marianine down to a chamber of death in the catacombs under Paris. There, as a kind of proto-Dracula, he plans to drain her "vital [mesmeric] fluid," using "his unusual voice...like that of the serpent who long ago seduced the first woman" to bring her to "a domain where no one enters without being at one and the same time both *dead*

---

1 *Blackwood's Edinburgh Magazine* (1817), p. 37.
2 *Blackwood's*, Jan., 1834, p. 471.

and *alive*." This quantum uncertainty lingers almost to the last page when Dr. Saint-Aubin, "interested in that science [mesmerism] whose wonders surpass the miracles of yore," uses his morally superior powers to wake her from her trance and snatch her just in time from the clutches of death.

Young Gervayse Pyncheon, in Hawthorne's *House of the Seven Gables* (1851), climbs onto his grandfather's knee only to discover to his horror that the old man is dead from a wizard's curse. Thomas Maule, one of several mesmerists in the novel, hypnotizes the daughter of a shady landowner and telepathically commands her to die. In Poe's "Mesmeric Revelation" (1850) the mesmerist known only as "P." has a philosophic dialogue with a subject he thinks is in a trance, but when he wakes him up, realizes he's been dead the whole time. In another Poe story, "The Facts in the Case of M. Valdemar" (1845), a man appears to be dead but is kept "alive" by a mesmerist ("P." again) for seven months. When the subject speaks, he says, "I am dead." The mesmerist brings him out of his trance, whereupon the subject instantly turns into "a nearly liquid mass of loathsome...detestable putridity."

The entire oeuvre of Henry James (creator of Dr. Tarrant, the hypnotic charlatan in *The Bostonians*) is peopled with characters either exerting or resisting the influence of someone else. He came up with a new twist on the hypno-death theme, which he gave away to George du Maurier, who used it in *Trilby* (1894), one of the most popular novels of the nineteenth century. Early in the story, young Trilby is warned about mesmerists: "They get you into their power, and make you...murder, steal...and kill yourself!" But she is a teenager, and we all know how teenagers respond to warnings from adults. As an aspiring vocalist, she needs help with her voice, so she turns—of course—to a dreadful mesmerist named Svengali, whose influence is so strong that she falls into a trance merely by looking at his photograph. He helps her with her voice by keeping her in a hypnotic trance for eight hours a day until her relatives say, "our Trilby [is] dead." In the concluding scene she sings her heart out at a recital while Svengali sits in the audience exerting his powerful control. Without her knowing it, he dies in his seat. When she discovers that Svengali is dead, she promptly dies herself, her vital essence drained by hypnotic predation.

Extending the physical distance of the mesmerist from the subject was a point of special interest long before Svengali's remote control of Trilby. Actual experiments were conducted in the telepathic broadcast of mesmeric commands from adjoining rooms, then the distance was progressively increased. Mesmeric proximity found its way into Poe's "Tale of the Ragged Mountains" (1844), where Bedloe is put in a trance and walks through a wilderness location that supposedly exists only in his mind. In this state of waking sleep, Bedloe witnesses the murder of a military officer and then experiences his own death by a poisoned arrow. When he awakens from his trance, he relates the experience to a mesmerist, Dr. Templeton, who happens to be writing an account of a real-life military officer's death that occurred at the same time and place Bedloe witnessed it in his hypnotic sleep. A week later Bedloe dies from the imagined lethal arrow.

In Elizabeth Gaskell's *Cranford* (1851), the stage magician, Brunoni, has a will of such "deadly force" that he can condense it into a single word powerful enough to kill a canary. It's possible that Gaskell tried to do in fiction what the actual hypnotist, Abbé José-Custodio de Faria, tried but failed to do at a party given by Chateaubriand in 1802: kill a canary with his mind. Later in the story another animal victim, a dog named Carlo, is almost killed in the same way. Arthur Conan Doyle's short story, "John Barrington Cowles" (1884), features a dog, also named Carlo, that is indeed finished off by the mesmeric power of a beautiful woman. Her influence also causes the death of three male humans.

Death by mental projection can be a two-way street, as Doyle describes in *The Parasite* (1894) where the evil mesmerist, Miss Penclosa, influences a young man to throw acid in the face of his fiancé. Before the assault can happen, the hyper-influential Penclosa dies of hypnotic over-exertion. I don't know if Conan Doyle knew how exhausting hypnotic practice can be, but from my own experience I can attest that from all the intensity of focus required to pull it off, it is an energy-draining endeavor. Later in his career, the Chicago hypnotist Edwin Baron, in presenting his show of exquisitely subtle skill, often collapsed afterward backstage.

By the end of the nineteenth century, fictional hypno-death gave way to the real thing. A hypnotized male subject in an 1891 medical demonstration was told he could not breathe. His respiration stopped for three minutes and it was "believed death could be caused unless the spell was removed," which it was, and none too soon.[1] The *New York Times* reported an experiment where a hypnotized subject obeyed the command to put arsenic in the food of a friend.[2] That was also stopped just in time. A Frenchman in Algeria, Henri Chambige, hypnotized his girlfriend, Madeleine Grille, apparently to shut her up in an argument. As a fixed, catatonic target he shot her in the head while still in a trance.[3] A Hungarian known only as Neukor hypnotized a young woman at a séance, and for entertainment purposes told her she had consumption. She shrieked and immediately fell dead.[4]

Laws and prohibitions worldwide against these kinds of stunts did not prevent a hypnotized girl from following the suggestion to point a loaded revolver at her mother and pull the trigger. She did not know the bullets were blanks. Nor did it keep a Belgian "professor" from hypnotizing a man before a live audience and telling him to murder his own father. The subject reported he "enjoyed killing him in cold blood."[5] Presumably with a rigged weapon.

Ivan Benedich, a Russian with control issues, repeatedly hypnotized the woman whose family would not let her marry him. Out of revenge he put her under and told her she had consumption. He hoped that when she began to show symptoms, the family would cease their objection to him, but they did not. So Benedich let her die of a disease that was nothing more than a suggestion planted in her mind.[6]

Causing death by hypnosis is one thing, getting away with it is another. It's commonly assumed that hypnotic

1 *New York Times*, Aug. 14, 1891.

2 *New York Times*, Aug. 14, 1891.

3 Martin Willis & Catherine Wynne, eds., *Victorian Literary Mesmerism* (1994), p. 203.

4 *New York Times,* Sep. 19, 1894.

5 *British Medical Journal*, Nov. 24, 1888, p. 1176, quoted in *Victorian Literary Mesmerism,* cited above 209.

6 *New York Times,* May 30, 1897.

suggestion is more mechanistic than it actually is. The hypnotic state (or whatever you want to call it) is more like a bubble than a lock. Yet attempts have been made to fortify that bubble. Perhaps the first attempt at what came to be called "psychic driving" (popularized in the *Manchurian Candidate*) was in 1894 outside of Winfield, Kansas. Thomas McDonald, under hypnotic control, was hiding in a tree as someone named Patton rode by on a horse. Given a posthypnotic command by an amateur hypnotist named Anderson Gray, he shot Patton dead.

The incident began when a neighbor transferred his entire estate to Gray so his wife would not get it in a divorce settlement. The understanding was that once the divorce was finalized, Gray would transfer the estate back. The greedy Gray, however, decided to keep it. Since Patton was the only witness to the secret deal, Gray figured that if he whacked Patton, the neighbor would have no witness and Gray could enjoy his ill-gotten enrichment.

At first Gray tried to hypnotize Patton to kill his own cousin (who was a better shot), hoping Patton would be killed in return. That got nowhere, so he recruited Thomas McDonald, who was a hypnotist's dream. After putting him in a deep trance, Gray told him that Patton was trying to seduce his wife, thus giving McDonald motivation to shoot him. After murdering Patton, the act would be erased from McDonald's memory. All went according to plan until McDonald's posthypnotic amnesia failed to hold. He confessed everything and the land-grabbing hypnotist was found guilty of murder while his programmed assassin went free.

Things did not turn out as well for another Manchurian Candidate, a janitor whose mind was taken over by Harry Hayward, known as "the Minneapolis Svengali." The same year that *Trilby* was a best-seller (1894) Hayward decided to use the janitor to terminate a dressmaker whom he had persuaded to take out two life insurance policies naming himself as beneficiary. After repeated conditioning, Hayward sent the janitor out one night to take the dressmaker on a relaxing horse and buggy ride around Lake Calhoun and shoot her in the head. The janitor carried out the command and dumped the dressmaker's body on the road. When the janitor was taken into custody he quickly snitched on his programmer. Whether Hayward actually used formal hypnotic techniques or "psychically drove" him through relentless repeated commands is not clear. At the janitor's trial "Dr." Herbert Flint, a stage hypnotist known for suggesting electrocution in his volunteers, was called as an expert witness. He easily hypnotized the janitor in his cell and testified he had "practically no mind" and could "easily be controlled." Unlike the Kansas assassin, the Minneapolis janitor got life in prison. As for the hypnotist, he was sentenced to be hung for murder.[1]

Having achieved nationwide notoriety, partly from piggy-backing on the current Svengali craze, Hayward saw an opportunity to extend his influence in the time he had left. From his jail cell he generated endless fictions about himself that were dutifully reported by the press and believed by the public. Actual evidence indicated he was a prolific serial killer, but in addition to his actual crimes he fabricated many more. He made himself a living snowstorm of untruth in which the public was eager to bury itself. As his day of reckoning approached, one account had him upholstering his scaffold in velvet. Another had him showing up for his execution nattily dressed in cutaway coat and pinstripe trousers, while another reported him dressed in a black robe and cap. *The Police Gazette* printed a false account of him eloquently reciting a long selection from Dryden's *Translations of the Odes of Horace* just as they pulled the trapdoor out from under him. (He actually did recite extensively from Dryden, but during a rambling confession in his jail cell.) His last words—jokes and all—were allegedly recorded on wax cylinders and sold to eager buyers. It was all an act, full of sound and fury, signifying nothing.

One could say Hayward was a little different. "A little different" is the wording often used by banquet planners who hire a hypnotist instead of a DJ no one sticks around for, or school principals looking for something other than the same old assembly program on drugs or self-esteem. Hypnotists are not—cannot—be part of the populace. They must always be "a little different." Westervelt in Hawthorne's *The Blithedale*

---

1 *New York Times*, April 7, 8, 1895.

Romance (1852) is a nomad with eyes that expose "something that ought not to be left prominent." Coverdale, the narrator, calls mesmerists "goblins of degraded death...outcasts, mere refuse-stuff." Balzac's Centenarian has "a smile worthy of Satan," and Doyle's Miss Penclosa only smiles "out of amusement" at the misfortune that she causes.

To emphasize their difference, hypnotists are physical anomalies too. The Centenarian is a giant, as is Svengali. Miss Northcott in Doyle's "John Barrington Cowles" stands out with her "extreme beauty," and his Miss Penclosa in *The Parasite* is a "creature with a crutch...a deformed woman." The physical quality that most differentiates them is the *eyes* (note the iconic image of Charles Manson's bulging peepers). A penetrating gaze indicates the uncanny intention of control, which is why hypnotists have been traditionally depicted in poses with an intense stare. Coleridge's Ancient Mariner holds the wedding guest "with his glittering eye," and Svengali's "big eyes" are "full of stern command." Light, necessary for vision, also plays a part: "eyes of fire," "eyes with an infernal and blinding light," "his flaming eyes," "a thread of light from his hollow eyes," etc. When Balzac's Centenarian meets his female victim, he focuses "the full beam of his eye." Hawthorne's Thomas Maule, "by the power of his eye" draws "people into his own mind"—before killing them. Doyle's Miss Penclosa has eyes that follow people with "serene confidence" until they fall under her fatal control. His Miss Northcott has a gaze so powerful it overrides and disrupts the powers of another hypnotist in the middle of a show, driving him from the stage.

If eyes capture attention, it's the voice that delivers the goods. Balzac's evil Centenarian has a voice like "the sound that issues from under an aqueduct," and when he insinuates it into the ear of Marianine, she's as good as gone. With the rapid evolution of amplified sound in the early twentieth century, the disembodied voice of a hypnotic predator went from an echo under an aqueduct to reaching masses. Erik Jan Hannusen's hypnotism shows at the Palace of the Occult in Berlin impressed Hitler, who would not have minded having some of that power for himself, enhanced by the world's first loudspeakers as well as radio. Some believe that he actually asked Hannusen for lessons in hypnotic control.[1] Although there's no direct evidence, it could have been possible. Whether he got lessons from Hannusen or not, the Fürer used the hypnotic techniques of both eye (focus on the swastika) and voice (amplified) to exert terminal control. Hannusen was eventually killed by assassins in Hitler's inner circle, not because he was Jewish, but because he was achieving too much influence over rival Nazi controllers.[2]

Any lie, no matter how preposterous, can become, as Balzac wrote in *Ursule Mirouët*, "charged...with magnetic fluid to penetrate the hearer at every pore." That could be deadly. We laugh off the old-fashioned bug-eyed, platinum-piped mesmerist hunting down victims one at a time, but not as easily as laughing off today's sophisticated means of deadly control by images (eye) and words (ear) broadcast through the mesmeric ether to TV and computer screens globally, influencing more minds on a greater scale than at any other time in human history. The end of the world will be a hypnotic event.

1 Richard Spence, *New Dawn* (June, 2014), "Erik Jan Hanussen: Hitler's Jewish Psychic," newdawnmagazine.com.

2 There is better evidence that Hitler was more impressed by Hanussen's appearing to predict the future. Any fake psychic knows that predictions are a matter of making a *lot* of them as well as keeping them sufficiently vague, aware that marks (dupes) will forgive the misses and use their imaginations to inflate the hits. Correctly predicting the Reichstag Fire (Feb. 27, 1933) was a little too big a hit for Hanussen. He was suspected of having something to do with it. See "Erik Jan Hanussen: Hitler's Jewish Psychic," Richard Spence, newdawnmagazine.com.

7 - Twins Joined at the Forehead: Hypnosis and TV

During the reign of King Louis XVI, it was all there: the broadcast, the set, the reception. Anton Mesmer's proto-television was called a *baquet* ("bucket").[1] As you touched the protruding metal rods (rabbit ears) of Mesmer's *baquet* (acting as the set), waves of "magnetic fluid" broadcast themselves into your head like yuks from a game show. The brain-buzz would set you laughing or massage you into lethargy, or just as likely drop you to the floor in convulsions. Women in petticoats and puffed overskirts rolled around and kicked up their legs. Men in waistcoats and knee breeches howled like dogs. A fee was involved.

Reactions before his studio audience were so novel and extreme, with all the fainting and shaking and howling, that by 1784 King Louis XVI ordered a commission to investigate. The King's commissioners questioned the magnetic fluid's potential effect on "sensitive women" who might go so far as to experience what they called "the sweetest emotion.""[2] With Enlightenment logic, they pondered the problem of how this control might affect "the involuntary instinct of imitation." People could forget their obedience to the Bourbon Monarchy (not to mention the Church) and start demanding liberty, equality, fraternity and all that sort of thing. Mesmer was eventually discredited and run out of town just before they wheeled in the guillotine, but it didn't cut off the power of his *baquet*.

While Mesmer was broadcasting animal magnetism from his nicely appointed studio in Paris, another kind of magnetism was going around—the electro kind—which would

---

1 A photo of the only known *baquet* still in existence can be seen at: founders.archives.gov/documents/Franklin/01-42-02-0304

2 Quoted in Alan Gauld, *History of Hypnotism* (1992), p. 28-29.

eventually energize the hypnotic *baquet* with something real and supersaturate the world with its magnetic confluence. As early as the 1720s, it was known that glass rods, similar to the rabbit ears sprouting from Mesmer's bucket, could be rubbed to pick up a charge and attract small objects. Benjamin Franklin got one and had a lot of fun with it.

Electromagnetic curiosity grew into popular stage shows featuring static explosions, sparkling spirals, luminescent flashes, and containers of bluish and greenish glows. In theaters like the Musée de Monsieur in Paris the public marveled at electric spinning wheels, chimes, and books with titles that lit up. Induction coils charged up the hair in huge, frizzed halos and threw twenty-foot arcs of lightening across the stage. Georg Mathias Bose, German professor of theology, invented a way to store enough static electricity that he could place a "very young boy" in a box and cause his entire body to be bathed in light like the baby Jesus. The Adelaide Gallery in London delighted an audience at one show by giving the Duke of Wellington such a shock that it left him "helpless as an infant." There was the charged-up king's crown that dealt a massive jolt to anyone attempting to remove it from the king's head. Women were charged with the new wonder juice and men given the go-ahead to try and kiss them, only to be rewarded by a giant spark to the face.[1] Despite warnings similar to those about mesmerism, the prevailing attitude toward electromagnetism remained one of crowd-pleasing amusement.

The first electric show performers were called "electricians," and the first hypnotists were called "magnetizers." They worked on separate stages, each demonstrating that the invisible force they worked with could be controlled from a distance. Electric people such as Luigi Galvani and Alessandro Volta considered Mesmer a crackpot because he wasn't scientific enough to quantify his way out of a bucket. Mesmer thought his skeptics just didn't get it. Benjamin

---

1 Linda Simon, *Dark Light* (2004), p. 21. Also, for electrical stage shows see Chapter 2, Iwan Rhys Morus, *Frankenstein's Children, Electricity, Exhibition, and Experiment in Early Nineteenth-Century London* (1998); and Marcello Pera, *The Ambiguous Frog, the Galvani-Volta Controversy on Animal Electricity* (English translation, 1992) pp. 6-16.

Franklin, adept as he was at clever tricks with his glass rod, was one of those skeptics called in by King Louis XVI to prove that Mesmer was a fraud. Interestingly, Mesmer and his detractors agreed on one thing: electricity and animal magnetism both traveled through a universal "ether." They also shared an identical symbol—the zig zag shape of a lightning bolt. This symbol of invisible influence appeared in 18th century lithographs of Mesmer's *baquet,* and continued to the first logos of RCA and NBC TV in the 1930s when the term "ether" was still used for the medium through which the zig zags traveled.[1] The symbol still emblazons the sides of electric repair trucks and emanates from the fingertips of hypnotists on their posters. This merge in the form of a symbol is expressed in the lines of Gjertrud Schnackenberg's *Throne of Labdacus* (2000):

> *...two masked figures*
> *Holding the broken halves of a prophesy*
> *Whose jagged seams they press together*
> *And see the shape of lightning.*

Prophesies come, as prophesies do, from nature. Animals have always made their prophetic presence. Images of horses and aurochs were first broadcast 17,000 years ago from the walls of Lascaux cave, although we'll never know their intended influence. Subjects magnetically influenced by Mesmer in the 1700s clucked and kicked like their phylogenetic counterparts. Animals made their prophetic presence in the labs of electricians. Franklin became so enthralled by electricity that after he moved on from the glass rod, he used five Leyden jars hooked up in series to kill a ten-pound turkey. "Birds killed in this manner," he wrote, "eat uncommonly tender."[2] Around the time Mesmer began his stage shows in Paris, Henry Cavendish built an artificial electric torpedo fish out of metal plates that put the whammy on anyone who touched it. Galvani found that if he touched the legs of a dead frog with a metal

---

1 Evan I. Schwartz, *The Last Lone Inventor, David Sarnoff vs Philo T. Farnsworth, a tale of Genius, Deceit, and the birth of Television* (2002), p.5.
2 Dayton Clarence Miller, *Sparks, Lightning, Cosmic Rays, an Anecdotal History of Electricity* (1939), p. 64.

probe, they would twitch, not unlike subjects who touched the antennas of Mesmer's *baquet*. When Galvani applied his metallic antennas to other hapless creatures relieved of their sentience, he got the same result. He concluded that a hidden force originated in the nerves of all living things and this conclusion became widely accepted. Show business wasted no time taking it on the road.

Entertainment was hard to come by in those days of TV's incipience and it didn't take much to please a crowd. One of the first galvanic twitch acts was Giovanni Aldini, whose routine consisted of sheep and pig heads whose eyes and snouts were stimulated to blink and grimace as if alive. As every entertainer knows, you have to keep coming up with new material, so Aldini went from dead animals to dead people, specifically executed criminals. When properly stimulated, their arms and legs moved as if they were alive, which was entertaining enough, but there was one problem. The guillotine deprived his subjects of a head. Since facial grimaces were the real crowd-pleasers, Aldini took his act to London where execution was by hanging, so he had a head to work with. Timing could not have been better on January 17, 1803 when George Foster was hanged for murdering his wife. Aldini managed to get permission to pluck Foster's body from under the scaffold and bring it up on stage at the Royal College of Surgeons. Everyone in the audience must have leaned forward in their seats as Aldini applied his probe to the dead man's face. His left eye suddenly opened! That alone would have closed any show, but Aldini didn't stop there. One can only imagine the gasps of shock and surprise as the galvanic probe touched Mr. Foster's rectum, resulting in such a whole-body convulsion that his cadaver nearly flew off the table, a reaction not altogether unlike that if Mr. Foster were still alive.[1] This uncanny animation of the non-living was widely sensationalized in the *London Times* and is said to have inspired Mary Shelley's *Frankenstein; or the Modern Prometheus,* published fifteen years later.

Galvani and his followers continued to believe that electricity originated in the organism itself. Then, in 1799,

---

1 André Parent, "Giovanni Aldini: From Animal Electricity to Human Brain Stimulation" in *Canadian Journal of Neurological Sciences* (Vol. 31, No. 4, 2004).

Alesandro Volta built an artificial electric fish out of silver and tin disks stacked in a moist medium similar to the arrangement of cells in the animal's electric shock organ. It was the first battery. From this experiment he made the shocking claim that electricity did *not* come from animals, but could be created artificially. By proving that electric fluid (often today still referred to as "juice") could come from within a manmade system, an ever-increasing complexity of devices followed.

Continuing on a separate but parallel path, the animal magnetizers made refinements of their own. They discovered that mesmeric "fluid" did not originate in the *baquet* anymore that electric "fluid" originated in living tissue. Emphasis shifted to the eye. Instead of touching the *baquet* (a cumbersome prop to carry around), magnetizers exerted influence by directing subjects to fix their gaze on something small enough to carry in the pocket: a watch, a pendulum, a glittering object. The mesmerist became the *baquet* and was able to travel faster and book more demonstrations in a shorter time, resulting in mesmerism spreading rapidly, like electricity, throughout the world.

In the late 1790s, only a few years after Mesmer's big-time gig in Paris, James Tilly Matthews foresaw the merge of the two magnetisms in a device he called the Air Loom, literally capable of broadcasting influence over a distance of up to a thousand feet.[1] Susceptible subjects did not have to touch the rabbit ears. They received signals over the airwaves which caused them to make "good sense appear as insanity." He described the workings of this imaginary device so minutely that some people believed it actually existed, even though Matthews was a patient at the Bethlam asylum for the insane in London. Reading John Haslam's 1810 description of the Air Loom is like reading a description of modern-day electronic media. The Air Loom's network was managed by a sixty-five-year-old Rupert Murdoch type named "Bill," or "The King," who controlled a crew of adepts solely for the purpose of

---

1 John Haslam, *Illustrations of Madness* (1810), pp. 30, 32, 80, 146, 157. See also Mike Jay, *A Visionary Madness, the Case of James Tilly Matthews and the Influencing Machine* (2014), p. 20, 146-148, 157.

broadcasting public "assailment." It's "magnetic warp" reached the brain in such a way that "the sentiments of the heart have no communication with the operations of the intellect." It "contrived to lift into the brain some particular idea, which fixes attention to the exclusion of other thoughts...and does not belong to the train of [one's] own cogitations." The result is a hypnotism stage show consisting of "foot-curving, lethargy-making, spark-exploding, knee-nailing, burning out, eye-screwing, sight-stopping, roof-stringing, vital-tearing, fiber-ripping," and finally the dreaded "lobster-cracking," where the effect works like a large pair of lobster-crackers on the brain, depriving the subject "of that volition which constitutes...a being responsible for his actions." Such an unmediated mental state, he warned, "ought not to be at large." Yet the "thought vultures" of Matthews' putative device have become as real as the machines that produce them today. Present day versions of "Bill the King" are running white supremacist and cult websites, encrypted terrorist cells, Qanon news channels, lizard people forums, Fox News, Channel One in Russia, and all the rest.

In 1817, two years after the death of Mesmer, the element selenium was discovered, and by 1872, when mesmerism had become a household word, it was found that light could visibly energize it. A TV screen was in the making. A mere eight years later there were already articles on "video-telegraphy" appearing in scientific journals. Then came the Russians and the pace quickened. Chekhov was just beginning to write plays when one of his countrymen, Paul Nipkow, patented a scanning mechanism called the "Nipkow disk" that fooled the eye into perceiving a series of static images as if they were in motion. In 1900 another Russian, Constantin Perskyi, coined the word "television." By 1911 two other Russians, Boris Rosing and Vladimir Zworykin, were the first to actually shoot and transmit an image through what was still called the "ether." In that same year a "history of television" had already appeared in a German textbook.[1]

---

1 Arthur Korn & Bruno Glatzel, *Handbuch der Phototelegraphie und Telautographie*, mentioned in Albert Abramson, *The History of Television, 1882-1941* (1987), p. 41.

While television was gestating in numerous laboratories around the turn of the century, suggestion and the means of delivering it was growing into a visual form that could be seen by many. It was no longer enough to simply *imagine* magnetic influence flowing into you from a big bucket, or the bulging eyes of a traveling mesmerist. By the 1890s moving pictures made it possible to project images to large audiences, such that a train looked like it was really coming at you, and a villain looked like he was really going to murder a defenseless maiden. These suggestions were so real compared to what came before, and caused such disruption in early theaters, that projectionists were often forced to stop the film and put a message up on the screen for people to settle down before the movie could continue. Audiences soon became used to the illusion, and the calm-down messages were no longer necessary. Under this internalized influence mass society began to imitate the fashions and gestures they saw on the screen and the change in social consciousness accelerated.

The old mesmerists, however, were not about to die off that easily. In 1923 Joseph Dunninger (later a popular 1950s TV psychic) performed the first radio broadcast of "long distance hypnotism" on a listener ten miles away in Long Island. The subject was instructed to "look directly into the horn of the radio," reminiscent of Mesmer's suggested focus on his bucket of magnetism. In no time he was "staring at the ceiling with unstaring eyes." Then Dunninger physically transported himself to the "unstaring" subject, stretched him between two chairs like a human plank, and jabbed him through the arm with a large needle.[1] At that moment, like Dr. Frankenstein's animated electrical product, the two magnetisms were allegorically stitched together.

By 1938, Orson Welles could use radio to suggest a real Martian invasion to twelve million listeners. No hypnosis show was necessary because the medium of radio had already become the hypnotist. Those on whom it worked went into such a panic that the Federal Communications Commission prohibited such overt suggestion from that point on.

---

1 *New York Times*, July 15, 1923.

Another old mesmerist from the horse and buggy days, Howard Klein, described as "Dr. Mesmer's star successor," managed to clip clop his way onto CBS's *Hobby Lobby* radio show in 1941. He worked his antiquated form of magnetism on subjects in the studio audience while the electromagnetic signal went out to untold thousands. Klein's hypnotic volunteers ate lemons thinking they were peaches and swatted imaginary mosquitoes. A reporter at the scene noted prophetically, "many radio listeners might qualify as hypnotized" and the "aggravated lethargy" could, by being broadcast, hypnotize a large part of the US population "in one fell coo [sic]."[1]

Quietly, behind the scenes, there was increasing competition to broadcast over a great distance not just a voice, but a moving picture that could be seen on a surface flat as the wall of a cave. For this to happen, one of those newfangled selenium screens had to be perfected. To energize such a screen required an enormous amount of light, which required an enormous amount of electricity. A side effect of all that energy was heat, so much that the human face could not stand more than a few seconds before the camera.

As the Jazz Age began, British inventor and notorious crackpot John Logie Baird worked intensely to broadcast facial contours under all that heat-generating light. Using technology from the previous century, Baird jerry-built a workable camera and TV from a hat box, glue, knitting needles and tape, then focused it on the famously uncomplaining Stookie Bill and burned away his entire face. No problem, because Stookie Bill was a ventriloquist dummy.[2] After his smiling visage was charred like a marshmallow in a campfire, a fresh Stookie was brought in. As late as 1937, TV studio lights were still so hot that Kansas City newscaster John Cameron Swayze had to take precautions so they would not burn off his eyebrows.[3]

Baird was so determined in his efforts to merge electromagnetism with the eye that he actually constructed a camera lens from a real human eyeball begged off a surgeon,

---

1 *Time Magazine*, Oct. 13, 1941, p. 55.

2 A full account is given in *Restoring Baird's Image*, Donald F. McLean (2000).

3 Michael Ritchie, *Please Stand By, a Prehistory of Television* (1994), p. 90.

but realized it was impractical for widespread commercial use.[1] Overcoming this and other false starts, he went on to construct various cameras until the heat problem, if not completely solved, became more or less manageable. On Tuesday, January 26, 1926 he invited forty members of the Royal Institution to his cramped quarters to witness the world's first public broadcast of a living human being. He used an 1884 Nipkow disk and a TV made from his usual assemblage of odds and ends (known as mechanical TV, soon to be eclipsed by electronic TV). Viewers were mesmerized by what they saw. One distinguished gentleman was so entranced that he leaned in too close to the spinning Nipkow disc that caught his beard and nearly pulled his face off.[2] Within a year Baird Television Network was transmitting daily programs from London.

In 1920, while Baird was trying to make a steampunk television out of glue, hatboxes and eyeballs, a fourteen-year-old farm boy and electrical hobbyist in Idaho directed his own eyeballs onto the field he was plowing and, as he was known to do, went into a trance. This time the trance was so deep that in a miraculous mental flash he saw in the lines of crops (variously reported as potatoes, beets or hay) the workings of electronic television. The kid's name was Philo Farnsworth. He was more than just a daydreamer. He drew a circuit diagram on a classroom blackboard to the utter astonishment of his science teacher. Then he built a working model in a shed. By the time he'd barely started shaving, he took out a series of patents. In 1934 he traveled to London to meet Baird and work out a deal with Baird Television Network, already broadcasting quite successfully, but with nineteenth century technology. When Baird first saw with his own *eyes* Farnsworth's technically superior version of transmitting moving images, he reacted, in the words of Farnsworth's wife, "like one mesmerized."[3] So mesmerized, in fact, that he gave Farnsworth $50,000 for the rights to use his modern improvement.

By 1939 the New York World's Fair featured Farnsworth's (not Baird's) TV to the public under the banner,

---

1 Evan I. Schwartz, *The Last Lone Inventor, David Sarnoff vs Philo T. Farnsworth, a Tale of Genius, Deceit, and the Birth of Television* (2002), p. 130.

2 *Tube*, cited above, p. 59.

3 *Please Stand By*, cited above, p. 28.

"All *eyes* to the future!" David Sarnoff of NBC radio wrote in the *New York Times* of a new "electric *eye*" to "scan the world."[1] While Farnsworth's electric eye was scanning the world from the Fair in New York, the Nazis (one of Baird's first customers) had already figured out how to use electromagnetic waves in the form of radio to influence the masses.[2] Their paramilitary unit, the SS, in charge of enforcing Nazi ideology, bore on their insignia the zig zags of two lightning bolts.

On December 20, 1946, twenty-three years after Dunninger's hypnosis by radio, Peter Casson conducted the first known induction of the hypnotic state via closed circuit television on five volunteers from the British Broadcasting Corporation. One onlooker in another room fell into a trance merely by watching the screen, "although Casson was not then addressing the viewing audience." As a result of this experiment, the BBC decided that because of "the consequent danger of hypnotizing viewers who might not have anyone at hand to wake them up, a hypnotic television broadcast would not be advisable."[3]

As "wireless chloroform," so called by the *New York Times*,[4] wafted over mass culture, there arose a new academic discipline known at the time as "social science," which meant, in certain applications, persuasion with the intention of compelling the largest number of people to do whatever you want them to do. The Yale Institute of Human Research became the center of this new enterprise and received huge corporate grants to focus on radio and TV advertising. Clark Leonard Hull was hired by the Institute and became indispensable to its projects. Hull was very good at focusing himself on just one thing to the exclusion of everything else. He never saw a rabbit hole he didn't want to go down. As a boy in a small Michigan town, he was captivated by a traveling evangelist and sat transfixed until the moment he was called to step forward and declare himself saved. For a while he even considered becoming a preacher. Instead, he went on to become a professor of

---

1 *New York Times*, November 18, 1928.

2 John Thompson, "Nazi TV, Television and its Influence on World War II" (historyofyesterday.com).

3 *The Oakland Tribune* (California), Dec. 20, 1946, quoted in Damon Clowne, *Hypnosis for Sabotage, a Study in Psychiatry* (1947), p. 6.

4 July 14, 1923.

experimental psychology at the University of Wisconsin, where his new fixation was the study of hypnotism.[1]

During his tenure at the Institute, he published numerous monographs on applied hypnosis, some in the *Journal of Abnormal Social Psychology.* In *Hypnosis and Suggestibility* (1933) he provided charts and mathematical formulas showing "the power of hypnotic suggestion to produce a transcendence of voluntary capacity."[2] His unwavering focus on producing behavior with reduced awareness was, as he wrote, "similar to the introduction of electricity." Demonstrations of his suggestive techniques at Yale were described as having "an electric effect." When other universities saw large grants going to Hull's Yale Institute, they began to copy his method of combining two "essential identities"—the conditioned reflex (measured with the mathematical precision of the electricians) and subconscious phenomena (described by Freud and based in part on his own early work with hypnotism).

Animals continued their ancient sacrificial role in the Institute's labs. They were treated to endless electric shocks, punishment grills, restraining devices, starvation, vivisection and mutilation in the name of engineering the influence of humans. To Hull, people in general were inherently disordered and in need of control. He felt the Institute should be dominated by a "Hitler type" and even proposed research in eugenics.[3] The first focus groups were created behind two-way mirrors to study humans as if they were lab rats. Hull's overwhelming success with manipulated behavior made him president of the American Psychological Association and, in the words of Rebecca Lemov in *World as Laboratory* (2005), "the most powerful behaviorist in the world."

In the 1950s, ten years after the British Broadcasting Corporation warned about showing hypnotism on television, stage hypnotist Ormond McGill reached an audience of millions

---

1 Biographical details from Frank A. Beach, *Clark Leonard Hull, a Biographical Memoir* (National Academy of Sciences, 1959).

2 Clark L. Hull, *Hypnosis and Suggestibility* (1933), p. 281.

3 J. G. Morawski, "Organizing Knowledge and Behavior at Yale's Institute of Human Relations" in *Isis*, (June, 1966), p. 234.

on Art Linkletter's *People Are Funny* show by making fools of his volunteers in front of a backdrop for Niblets Mexicorn. As you enjoyed someone else's hypnotic delusions projected from a *baquet* in your living room, that enjoyment was paired, via Hull's research, with a corporate product. The *baquet* was full of the sweetest mesmeric fluid—money.

By eyeing the selenium bucket, millions of hypnotic puppets fell into ever more carefully engineered trances. Everything King Louis's Royal Commission was concerned about came to be. The "power of imitation" fissioned into the ubiquitous spread of magnetic unreality. Then the influence itself took over and transcended the influencers. John Logie Baird, who introduced television broadcasting to the world, died in obscurity. When Philo Farnsworth, inventor of electronic TV, went on the "I've Got a Secret" show in 1957, no one recognized him. For stumping the panel as to who he was, he walked away with $80 and a carton of Winstons.[1] Edward R. Murrow, who achieved much of his fame through TV, eventually denounced it for its "decadence, escapism, and insulation from the realities of the world." Newton Minow, chairman of the Federal Communications Commission (FCC) declared TV a "vast wasteland." When asked which of his many inventions was most essential to electronic television, Vladimir Zworykin could have said the photocell, the iconoscope picture tube, or the cathode ray transmitter, but said "the switch" so he could "turn the damn thing off."[2]

But it was more likely the damn thing would be left on. By the time television engulfed cinema, audiences were so swallowed by the suggestion industry that what they saw was not just a representation of reality, but reality itself. And from there it was a seamless transition to the computer screen, where visual and audio suggestions stream into minds with a directness never seen before. Once in, there is no getting out because there is no outside. The screen is not only reality itself, it is *consciousness* itself. In 1928, when Philo Farnsworth demonstrated the first electronic TV to investment bankers, one of them said, "When are we going to see some dollars in this thing?" Farnsworth then proceeded to

1 *The Last Lone Inventor* cited above, p. 292.
2 *The Last Lone Inventor* cited above, p. 293.

flash a dollar sign on the screen and the deal was done.[1] We are walking hypnotic targets for someone else's profit. And for large numbers of these targets, the stage show they are in features false information, conspiracy theories, pathological incitements, and the wholesale annihilation of rational thought.

The zig-zags of animal magnetism have shot directly from Mesmer's *baquet* to the remote control in your hand to the buds in your ear. The universal ether is now the universal media, a complete head-to-head graft of the animal with the electro, creating a worldwide hypnotic reality. It is pure trance. Ultimate trance. As real as the Orson Welles Martian invasion for those to whom it did not occur to change the station.

---

1 Ibid. p. 135.

8 - Those People: Hate and the Hypnotic Other

Hate is such an available and immediate natural resource that exploiting it, to those so inclined, is as irresistible as oil on native land. There are many standard stunts in the hypnotist's repertoire for extracting it from volunteers for comical situations. More than other stage scenarios, once the hate routine is started, it can be difficult to stop. It has to be used with caution. I know of at least two Las Vegas hypnotists who do the stunt where a male subject is sent back to the audience with a posthypnotic trigger word. Upon hearing the trigger word (such as his name mispronounced) the subject rushes back to the stage "hopping mad" as told to do. Suspense builds as the angry subject accosts the hypnotist. Just as he is about to take a swing, the hypnotist yells "Sleep!" and the subject drops to the floor. Big laugh. Terry Stokes told me that one time the sleep command didn't work and the angry subject *did* knock his block off. Even bigger laugh.

Once subjects are hypnotized and have successfully responded to other suggestions such as ants in their pants or their mouths stuck open, the stage is set for the release of hate. I use the standard suggestion that on the count of three, subjects will find their bellybuttons missing. *Someone took them! And they say they won't give them back!* Any other body part will do, depending on the taste level of the audience, but the bellybutton is more broadly acceptable. Without questioning its absurdity, subjects will probe the relevant area as anger rises, although what is supposed to be gone is obviously still there. Further incitement is easy and happens virtually on its own.

Would you like to know who took them?

Damn right they would.

I'll tell you... but, YOU CAN'T GET OUT OF YOUR CHAIRS!

This latter command has to be stressed in no uncertain terms because when I point to the innocent "culprit" in the front row, rage focuses to such a burning heat that subjects struggle like dogs on a chain to escape their chairs. I ask each one, *What do you think about THAT PERSON now?* They respond with varying degrees of indelicacy and *escalating hate*, much to the audience's amusement. Contrary to their waking personalities, they make throat-cut gestures and shout chilling curses at the accused. Their sense of injustice can be so strong that individuals may break free of their chairs in spite of my command to stay seated and charge toward the "guilty" one ready to knock his block off. It takes a very authoritative follow-up command to get them to sit back down, sometimes with physical restraint. Nobel poet Wisława Szymborska did not have to know about this specific situation to write, "hatred commands, / for hatred's got it down."

Arousing hate through suggestion can even be directed to an inanimate object. If I show a paper cup held with a pair of tongs and say, *this cup is vile and untouchable*, no one will touch it, even if I fill it with glass beads and say are diamonds they can have for free. The vileness could just as easily be in the form of a paperclip, a speck of dust—or a category of person. I can produce a balloon with a smiley face and say to a selected subject, *this is the cause of everything bad that's ever happened to you.* To the other subjects I say, *When he does what he has to do, CHEER HIM ON!*

After the subject bats at the hated balloon to the audience's delight, the moment of violent catharsis occurs when it's squeezed and popped. Subjects shout their approval and the audience bursts into unstoppable laughter and applause.

To convince people in a heightened state of suggestibility that someone took their bellybuttons is a conspiracy theory in miniature, no different from the so-called "Great Replacement" delusion widely accepted by white supremacists who claim "white people" are being "replaced" by those who are not. Vanishing bellybuttons, vanishing white people, in both cases evidence to the contrary makes no difference. After surviving the holocaust, German philosopher Ernst Cassirer wrote in his last work, *The Myth of the State* (1946), that modern life with its advanced technology and apparent rationality is only the "upper layer of a much older stratum that reaches down to a great depth." Lurking in those depths is a reservoir of primitive fear that can be roiled with the stir stick of hate.

In the same post-War period Erich Fromm, in *Escape from Freedom* (1949), identified the suggestive stir stick as cultural stress, usually economic in nature. What could make a German citizen more fearfully insecure than having to pay 900% interest on a car loan in 1923[1] and then losing their job? That in itself was not a delusion, but hanging the blame on innocent parties was. As Fromm put it, "Nazism is radical opportunism." The same could be said of any influence in staged form.

For hate to be released from its primal stratum, a manipulator, according to Cassirer, must "know the magic spells," and become "the master of everything." It sounds familiar enough to me as one who works "spells" for a living. Rev. Wesley Arthur Swift, who died in 1970, used spells from the pulpit to create the skit known as "Christian Identity" to stir up hate and violence against Jews and Blacks. As spiritual leader of the Antelope Valley chapter of the Ku Klux Klan in California, he successfully spread suggestions of hate and bigotry through audiotapes and a network of traveling ministers trained in the same set of spells. People were "radicalized," or "hypnotized," whatever term you want to use. One of Rev. Swift's best subjects was Samuel Holloway Bowers, Jr., who became Imperial Wizard of the White Knights of the Ku Klux Klan in Mississippi, the most violent Klan group in America at the time.[2] "Professor" Frank Farnsworth, notorious for killing a subject on stage in a reckless hypnosis stunt (see Chapter 1) went on to become "King Kleagle" of the Ku Klux Klan in Maine and used his persuasive talents to increase the membership at rate of 1,000 per week.[3] All those influencers got plenty of attention with their stage shows of hate. But no laughs.

---

1 *Foundation for Economic Education* (fee.org) and *The Economist*.

2 Stuart Wexler, *America's Secret Jihad, the Hidden History of Religious Terrorism in the United States* (2015), p. 359.

3 *Boston Globe*, March 15, 1926.

In the 1960s Chicago hypnotist Edwin Baron did a skit where he told his subjects they were in a monster movie. *They are coming!* he warned, *The Gorilla, The Giant Spider, The Blob, THE INVADERS ... Fight them off!* For an element of righteousness, he added, *Save that girl!* Since invasions have to be met with force, especially when a "girl" is involved, Baron's subjects furiously flailed and punched the air at the despised—and imaginary—"invaders" while the audience went crazy. In one year alone Donald Trump ran over 2,000 Facebook ads that used the word "invasion."[1] When Patrick Crusius went into a Walmart in El Paso and killed twenty-two people, most of them Mexicans, he was acting out the suggestion planted in his mind by certain people in power that they were "invaders."[2] The same suggestion took hold in the mind of Dylann Roof, who thought African Americans were "taking over our country."[3] By murdering nine Black "invaders" in their Bible study group at Emanuel African Methodist Episcopal Church in Charleston, he thought he was "saving the white race," white women in particular (*Save that girl!*). Shortly after the massacre, *The Daily Beast* published an article titled "How I Escaped Becoming Dylann Roof." The author recalls as a teenager someone he repeatedly refers to as "my racist Svengali" tried to convince him to burn down the house of "black invaders" of his neighborhood. He was "fortunate" and "came to his senses" before he acted out Svengali's suggestion.[4]

Asked where the invasion idea came from, Roof's answer was, "It's all there on the internet." Alexandra Stern at the University of Michigan confirmed Roof's statement in *Proud Boys and the White Ethnostate,* with evidence showing that ninety percent of the white supremacy movement happens online in "shadow sites" like Gab and Bitchute, as well as a myriad of Facebook pages that proliferate faster than they can be taken down.[5]

---

1 *Public Discourse*, August 11, 2019 (thepublicdiscourse.com).

2 "Our European comrades don't have the gun rights needed to repel the millions of invaders that plaque [sic] their country," *Washington Post*, August 4, 2019.

3 *Police Chief Magazine* (policechiefmagazine.org).

4 *Daily Beast*, Apr. 14, 2017 (thedailybeast.com).

5 Alexandra Stern, *Proud Boys and the White Ethnostate* (2019), p. 95.

The mesmeric fluid of the internet's *baquet* dissolves everything it touches, good, bad and ugly. Its influence intensifies, captures and controls more powerfully than all the mesmerists who have ever lived combined. At the exact moment the Web helped Barack Obama win the presidency, the neo-Nazi website Stormfront.org overloaded with so many hits that it crashed.[1] When Tywanza Sanders was supposed to be participating in his Bible group in Charleston, he could not resist playing with his smartphone to upload a video of himself to Snapchat. In the background of that video was none other than Dylann Roof himself who, in a matter of moments, would pull out a Glock 41 .45-caliber handgun and murder Sanders and eight others.[2] Before the shooting began, Roof had done some uploading of his own, a racist rant to the website 8chan,[3] which was linked to at least three other violent hate crimes.

Australian hate recruit, Brenton Tarrant, became the very incarnation of the internet itself. According to a relative he had a "severe addiction" to video games. He carried his internet entrancement to a new level by purchasing a helmet-mounted Go Pro camera and linking it to the Facebook Live application. As he massacred fifty-one people at two mosques, he streamed the event in real time for seventeen minutes. The online environment of the World Wide Web was so "electrified" (i.e. "mesmerized") by the atrocity that within twenty-four hours it was viewed 1.5 million times globally. The chat platform *Discord* posted 40,000 messages. A right-wing personality on YouTube read Tarrant's manifesto to 600,000 subscribers. Almost immediately after the attack, Tarrant's admirers PhotoShopped his face onto the images of medieval saints and put them on T-shirts, tote bags and mugs marketed—where else?—on the internet. Designers of violent video games spliced live footage of the massacre into their digital amusements, also

---

1 Eli Saslow, *Rising out of Hatred, the Awakening of a Former White Nationalist* (2018), p. 10.

2 Jelani Cobb, "Inside the Trial of Dylann Roof" in *New Yorker,* January 29, 2017.

3 Patrick Lucas Austin, "What Is 8chan, and How Is It Related to This Weekend's Shootings? Here's What to Know," in *Time,* August 5, 2019.

marketed online.[1] The New Zealand government put together a Royal Commission of Inquiry into the Terrorist Attack on Christchurch Mosque similar to King Louis XVI's Royal Commission Report on Animal Magnetism. In both cases restrictions were recommended, and in both cases were minimally effective, if at all.[2]

There is no greater trance inducer than music, the reason it's constantly piped like mesmeric fluid into our ears by commercial interests paired with suggestions to *buy*. Hypnotists incorporate it into their routines to manipulate subjects into thinking they are disco dancers, famous singers, or to perform ridiculous acts like scratching their heads (or some other part of the body) to the beat of a popular ditty. "At heart it's really the music," writes Michael Kimmel in *Healing from Hate*, "that pulls young men in [to white supremacy]."[3] Fans unable to attend white power music concerts can watch them streaming live on the internet. Until recently, a website, aptly named *Micetrap*, offered a vast inventory of music albums by hatecore bands such as Screwdriver, Midtown Bootboys, Centurion, and Odin's Law, and streamed them twenty-four hours on its own radio station.[4] Two prepubescent girls known as the Gaede Sisters marketed their childlike innocence on folk-pop albums in praise of racial holy war. Michael Page, who in 2012 killed six at a Sikh Temple in Wisconsin, played bass guitar in several hate bands, and Christian Picciolini (since reformed into an anti-hate activist) was front man for the group that called itself Final Solution.[5]

Techniques other than music are used on the internet to induce the racist trance. Stormfront.org features chat rooms for parents on how to indoctrinate their kids into white supremacy

---

1 Graham Macklin, "The Christchurch Attacks: Livestream Terror in the Viral Video Age," in Combating Terrorism Center website (West Point), July, 2019 (ctc.usma.edu). Long and meticulously researched article with 172 footnotes from reliable sources in several languages.

2 "Is Social Media a Positive or Negative Influence on New Zealand's Democracy?" *UKEssays* (Nov. 2018). ukessays.com.

3 Michael S. Kimmel, *Healing from Hate: How Young Men get into—and out of—Violent Extremism* (2018), p. 155.

4 Tricia L. Nadolny, "South Jersey Seller of Hate Music Says he is Shutting Down to Find 'Self Peace'" in *Philadelphia Inquirer*, posted August 21, 2017 (inquirer.com).

5 *Healing from Hate*, cited above, p. 157.

through hate-themed puzzles, cartoons and coloring pages. Neo-Nazi dating sites like Whitedate.net ("to connect white supremacists seeking to preserve the future of the white race"), and WASP Love ("white nationalism") help fellow haters get together romantically. Those who do settle down together can enhance their domesticity with programs like the German-based *Balaclava Kuche*, a Nazi vegan cooking show. ("This account has been terminated due to multiple or severe violations of *YouTube*'s policy prohibiting hate speech.")

What is most obvious in a hypnotism demonstration is the subject's complete unawareness of what he or she is doing, no matter how absurd, such as laughing at an inflight comedy movie in a space ship to Mars. Dylann Roof's defense lawyer described him as so enthralled by internet sites that he could not distinguish the real world from the virtual one. A reporter for *The New Yorker* observed that Roof was someone who had not fully realized what he had done, like my hypnotic subjects with no awareness of having thought their shoe was a telephone. In his closing statement Roof remarked, "I felt like I had to do it. I still feel like I had to do it." Those words mimic subjects on stage who say, post-performance, they felt they "had to" do what I suggested even though they didn't know why.

That the mind can be swayed to see an absurdity as a truth appears to be an evolutionary design flaw. If we say that illusion is built into sentience, we should also say that uncertainty is built into illusion. Tricks can fail. Trances can break. Hypnotists know that distractions are always lurking to botch up their work. The show may go along promisingly until a subject, for some reason—a noise, a voice, someone bumping them—will break their trance. Dismissal from the stage follows. A white supremacist may wake up one morning and realize that blowing up a church doesn't feel right anymore. Failure to fall in line can result in dismissal from the fellowship in ways not altogether cordial.

When Angela King decided to let the good times roll one night at a Nazi shindig, she and some other party-goers let things get out of hand, trashing a bar, beating a young woman unconscious, and robbing an adult video store because they thought it was owned by a Jew. Police put an end to their fun and she was sent to prison. There she began to realize that some of her fellow inmates were of the same ethnic minorities she had previously sworn to exterminate. She was surprised by how well they treated her. With plenty of time to think, she began to change her mind about things. Eventually she became one of the founders of Life After Hate, an organization for rehabilitating white supremacists like herself.

Jackie Arklöv from Sweden, wanted for war crimes committed as a Croatian mercenary in the Bosnian War, thought he could take over the Swedish government and run it himself, like Charles Manson once tried to do in America. To fund this delusion, Arklöv staged a series of bank robberies ending with the murder, execution style, of two policemen. In prison he woke from his trance and began to reflect. As time went on, reflection turned to awareness, and awareness led to remorse. He wrote long, agonizing letters of apology to the widows of the policemen he murdered and is now spending the remaining fifteen years of his sentence (this is Sweden, not the US) studying Kant, Husserl and Wittgenstein. Upon release he hopes to work with the organization EXIT that de-trances neo-Nazis.

One of the more prominent names in this small but growing world of far-right apostasy is ex-Nazi musician Christian Picciolini. In an interview for *The Atlantic* he explains how he was lured into the movement by supremacist websites that used a "parallel process" employed by ISIS to target those who live most of their lives online "without real-world connections." It is precisely this lack of real-world connection that makes hypnotic subjects so entertaining when they start following suggestions of increasing absurdity. For whatever reason, Picciolini began to separate himself from the digital *baquet*. He cut his connections to white supremacy websites and re-established himself with the real world. In this new world he encountered erstwhile racial enemies who "showed me compassion at a time in my life when I least deserved it."

But people coming out of toxic trances are not well tolerated by those who induce them. Picciolini was subjected to harassment and death threats. In spite of persecution by those still "under," he is active in the Free Radicals Project to help other neo-Nazis come out of it. Besides Picciolini, Arklöv and King, there are enough white supremacists waking up from their trances to sustain the *Journal of Deradicalization*. From his perspective as a former deep insider, Picciolini sees violent neo-Nazi "subjects" (note the term) like Timothy McVeigh (169 deaths in Oklahoma City) or Anders Brievek (77 deaths in Norway) not as loners but "part of a larger ecosystem." He claims to know people in politics and law enforcement who are secretly white supremacists, and asks the ominous question whether there might be white-nationalist truckers and airline pilots. In spite of growing defections, he says, "It's going to get worse before it gets better."

"De-platforming [hate websites] is good," according to Picciolini, because "it makes people harder to reach," but hypnotic focus on the computer screen is a phenomenon we seem condemned to live with. Sites like 8chan and Stormfront have been described as "the heads of a hydra" and removing them does not eliminate the *baquet* itself, nor the reservoir of hate that lurks in the human subconscious. At the end of *American Swastika*, Pete Simi and Robert Futrell question whether the white power movement could ever be eliminated by dismantling their digital structures. "We do not have definitive answers." Complete de-platforming would involve the impossible task of uncoupling animal magnetism (suggestion) from electro magnetism (the means to implement it on a mass scale). King Louis XVI's Royal Commission tried its best to nip Mesmer in the bud, but the problem has only grown exponentially.

Even though awakened and dismissed from the stage, a subject may spontaneously slip back into a trance. To stay "wide awake and out of it" can be as difficult as "sleep and keep sleeping." It's not uncommon for me to re-hypnotize a subject and then wake them up a second time with the emphasized suggestion they are now awake and will *remain that way* "refreshed and relaxed and feeling better than ever before." Steven Wiegand, founder of *Micetrap*, came to a realization that selling large volumes of Nazi merchandise "caused pain to others." He declared he would no longer associate with the white supremacist movement. Although he wanted to start a reformed life, he found himself in a peculiar dilemma. He needed money, and at the same time he was stuck with a huge inventory of Nazi flags, T-shirts, hatecore music and Hitler knickknacks. He wrote on his website, "I am currently offering a sort of mystery box, you contact me and let me know how much you are looking to spend, a general idea of what you would like and also list anything you definitely do not want... Guaranteed, you will be extremely happy with everything you receive." He added ambiguously, "I've even received a few e-mails claiming to be from organizations looking to purchase massive quantities to burn. I tell you all the same thing, I don't care what you do with whatever you buy." He told the *Philadelphia Inquirer*, "I'm not a bad person, I'm not a bad person."

I was once persuaded, quite reluctantly, to do a pro bono hypnosis session with a woman who had seen my show and wanted me to help her overcome a dreadful fear of anything with wings, in particular fruit flies. When I entered her house, I saw that she was a hoarder, with the characteristic narrow pathways through canyons of junk. As we sat down at a large dining table piled with unwashed glasses and plates, a cloud of fruit flies wafted up, causing her to furiously swing her hands through the air to make them go away. Before we began, she pushed aside heaps of scrap to show me a small scratch on the table. She wanted to impress me with how she could rub a walnut shell onto the scratch to make it disappear, which it slightly did. She ignored the much larger problem of living in a landfill of her own making.

I failed to cure her phobia.

9 - Mesmer Made Me Do It: Mass Murder in Schools

The standard image of a teen is a sitting, standing or walking figure looking down at something in the hand. That something is the hand-held *baquet*. It's estimated that teenagers spend nine hours a day staring at a screen. That's the average. In some cases, it can be much more. Looking at one while driving accounts for three thousand teen deaths a year in the US, proving the *baquet's* magnetic predominance over life itself.[1]

In their mutually entangling dance through the generations, the paired magnetisms, animal and electro, have found themselves, among other places, in schools. Traditionally schools have been one of the most fertile venues for influence, a stage where everyone performs. It begins in kindergarten, where commands are given, as if by a mesmerist, and acting them out is expected without question. Children are told to take their places. They're made to hold hands and walk in circles. They're compelled to sing for an audience that does not exist. Their cultured response to suggestion develops into recitations and performances, as well as dangerous sport competitions.

The audience at the school venue is mostly each other. As in the hypnosis exhibition, convincingness is everything and fakes are treated none too kindly. Students fortunate enough to be dealt the right cards—physical wherewithal, social adroitness—are lucky. They are accepted, even popular. But those with a losing hand may fall victim to the Great Maurice's of the student body, as at Columbine High, where they were body slammed, pushed, punched and ordered to entertain crowds by being shoved across a floor covered with baby oil

---

1 As of Jan. 31, 2023. thezebra.com/resources/research/texting-and-driving-statistics/

and slide like a bowling ball into other losers.[1] They were made to push pennies across the floor with their nose[2] But victims used as entertainment by bullies are known to upstage their controllers.

After giving up nightclubs in the early 1970s I worked for School Assembly Service out of Chicago, traveling a thousand miles a week across ten Midwestern states for thirty-six weeks, performing at two to four schools per day. I also toured through Dakota Assemblies, affiliated with North Dakota State University in Fargo, and appeared at a majority of all the high schools in the Dakotas as well as parts of Montana, Nebraska and Minnesota. I saw more schools in a week, certainly a month, than most teachers and administrators see in a lifetime. A salesperson set up the route a year in advance, going from town to town, calling on schools and scheduling me as well as folk singers, whistlers, jugglers and magicians, preferably with an educational "message," however lame. It was openly understood that in spite of their alleged "educational value," assemblies were merely an excuse to get out of class and burn off some steam, especially in the winter. My program of turning students into Martians and meowing cats was sold as "Mind in Action." For this I received sixty dollars per appearance, but out of this came two twenty percent commissions, one to the salesperson, the other to the agency. I covered my own expenses. Pay-wise, it was about the same as filling in between stripper sets at nightclubs.

Because of bureaucratic, social, and disciplinary obstacles, assembly agencies stayed away from large cities, but did well in suburbs, where the schools had a new building smell and were situated on sprawling grounds with a sports field and bleachers with banks of floodlights, often carelessly left on over the weekend, wasting kilowatts of electricity. The kids in these schools were robust, healthy-looking, and well-dressed.

---

1 Louise I. Gerdes, ed., *Perspectives on Modern World History, the Columbine School Shooting* (2012), p. 87ff.
2 Rob Merritt and Brooks Brown, *No Easy Answers: The Truth Behind Death at Columbine* (2002), chap. 12. Full text at booksvooks.com.

Schools in smaller towns often had kindergarten through twelfth grade in the same crumbling building built early in the century with its unlevel wooden floors, musty smell, and buckets strategically placed to catch leaking water. In these schools the kids were smaller and not as well-dressed. In the most isolated towns, they were actually malformed from what looked like inbreeding. They'd enter the small gym as lurching mutants with expressions of profound blankness, ears oddly placed and eyes too far apart. As in night clubs, I had to take on all comers.

At every school, the principal was my contact person. They could be warm and gracious or cold and aloof. It was not uncommon for a principal to book a year's worth of assemblies and then be replaced with a new principal who didn't believe in them. He (they were virtually all "he") thought school should be work and no fun. But he had to honor the contract signed by his predecessor. These anti-assembly types had the teachers herd their classes into the gym, often not even knowing why. Then the principal went back to the office and the teachers went to their break room to smoke and gossip, leaving me to babysit the students until the next bell rang. Halfway through my presentation the principal might stick his head in the door and see an unruly mob, which only reinforced his bias against assemblies in the first place. On the report card that went back to the agency, he might maliciously write, "Couldn't control the students."

Other principals regarded the assembly as an educational experience in the long-standing tradition of the traveling Chautauquas, where speakers and entertainers went from town to town presenting programs of general interest. Before introducing me, they gave a short lecture, warning about booing, cheering and stomping feet. There would be no tolerance for heckling or throwing of anything. Appreciation was to be shown by applause only. The teachers kept a close watch on their pupils, and any miscreants were yanked from their seats and thrown out. On the report sheet sent back to the agency after every show, these schools were more likely to make comments like "well-received," or even "one of the best this we've had."

After a while they all merged together into one big school. One big stage. One big stress. This went on for years. My more successful performances introduced the entire school to a new reality, where all the rules with behavior were replaced with what should not be. Instead of sitting quietly and listening to the teacher, as years of conditioning had trained them to do, they became ducks and human wash machines. No classroom disruption could top that. Such extreme erasure of normalcy disturbed some teachers who resented their authority being so totally co-opted. The outside community might hear reports—grossly distorted of course—about what happened and sometimes not accept it as anything other than conjuring up the Devil. But up ahead were stranger, more overwhelming forces none of us could foresee.

It happened so slowly I didn't realize it at first. Reactions to my school assembly program became incrementally more subdued. Heckling and misbehavior slightly diminished, but so did the all-out hysteria. Then demand itself declined. Four hundred agency-booked appearances a year went down to three hundred. Over the course of several years, it dropped to half of that, and then half again. School assembly agencies themselves went out of business one by one. With agencies gone—and the performers they provided—schools gave in to no-cost programs by military recruiters and religious proselytizers. The administrative process changed to one where principals receded into the background. They no longer wandered among their students like a shepherd tending their flock. Decisions about assembly programs were delegated to student committees working under advisors, thus making the booking process more complicated and time-consuming. All pretense of educational message was gone and the student committees were more likely to spend limited funds on local boy bands popular on their Facebook pages.

I began to see more television monitors in halls and lunchrooms, and more computer terminals replacing bookshelves in the school library. And everywhere more heads looking down, not at books, but hand-held at gizmos. At first, I told subjects to turn them off before I began so their ring tones would not disturb the hypnotic procedure, but that became as impractical as telling everyone put away their shoes. I was being replaced by a whole new *baquet*.

In September of 1973 Dakota Assemblies booked me at Kyle, South Dakota on the Pine Ridge Indian Reservation. The previous February two hundred members of the American Indian Movement had occupied Wounded Knee at gunpoint for seventy-one days. The grievance was long-standing tribal corruption as well as the 1890 massacre of three hundred Lakota by the US Army. The wasicu (non-Indian) sheriff in nearby Murdo saw my out-of-state license plates and stopped me to ask what I was doing in town. I told him I had an assembly program scheduled in Kyle.

"I'm going to warn you not to go there. Soon as you get on the reservation, they'll run your car off the road and steal everything you've got. You'll be lucky they don't kill you."

I went there anyway and did my usual program for a group of two hundred elementary and high school kids. When I returned to my car afterward, I noticed I had inadvertently left the trunk open, but no one disturbed a thing, even though it was surrounded by students milling around at lunch hour. I returned to Kyle several times since, as well as Wounded Knee and schools on the Standing Rock, Cheyenne River, Rosebud, Sisseton and Flandreau Santee reservations. I hypnotized Ho-Chunk in Wisconsin and Navajo in Arizona. There were the Kickapoo, the Ojibwe, the Cherokee. Besides their school and tribal events, I performed at their casinos. No one ever ran me off the road or robbed me.

I did learn that Native Americans have their own way of responding to stage hypnotism. They are curious—or they would not have booked me in the first place—but they present a challenge arising from a cultural proclivity not to draw attention to themselves individually. If that happens, they shrink down into themselves in shyness. It's something I have to work with and the results are sometimes minimal, but Native groups are always unusually appreciative afterward, and my re-booking rate with them has always been high.

The first time I appeared at Navajo Community College in Tsaile, Arizona it was for an evening program open to the public. I could not get a single volunteer. I used every strategy I knew, but the stage remained empty except for myself. Without hypnotic subjects there is no hypnosis show, so I had no other option but to end my presentation in one of those extreme humiliations this profession is prone to. I stammered out some sort of explanation to the Student Activities Director who was just as dismayed as I was. After a few minutes of wrangling in my mind over how to handle the issue of my paycheck, I looked out on the stage, still lit up, and to my astonishment saw all the chairs filled with volunteers. I was at a loss as to what was happening, but I had no time to ponder, so I seized the moment and went back out to continue my demonstration in the usual manner. But another problem awaited me. There was no reaction from the audience. Human wash machines, nothing. Ants in the pants, nothing. This was just as puzzling to me as no one volunteering, but all I could do was muddle on. Then suddenly and inexplicably, as if a switch had been flipped, the audience started laughing at the point where the subjects, on my suggestion, started meowing like cats. They continued laughing all the way to the end. In my interaction with the students afterward I pieced together an explanation for why no one volunteered at first. Concern had spread throughout the tribal lands about a "white man who puts people to sleep" (there is no word in Navajo for "hypnotist"). They were associating me with "skin-walkers," evil entities in the tribal belief system, that could steal someone's soul.

When I initially left the empty stage in what I thought was defeat, there was no longer formal attention on anyone, so at that point volunteers felt more free to come up since no show was going on. Explaining the lack of reaction to the stunts, the Student Activities Director told me that an ancient medicine man, with a face weathered like a network of gullies, came in from the mountains to see the "white man who puts people to sleep." Because he carried so much prestige, everyone kept a close watch on him for guidance in case any soul-stealing might go on. I was told that no one had ever seen him smile, much less laugh, but when the subjects started meowing like cats, it struck him as so funny that he doubled over in laughter. That was enough to break the floodgates. Now it was okay to laugh. My influence was established. Their souls were safe.

Perhaps not that safe. When I returned several years after 9/11, I noticed a change in this remote, mystical place in the Chuska Mountains, where I'd always seen students in the traditional dress of deerskin moccasins and turquoise silver concho belts. This time the girls had cut their hair and dyed it green and red and pierced their nostrils and eyebrows with steel rivets. Boys sported tattoos and wore capacious jeans lowered halfway down their buttocks. The audience was smaller than before, with a lot of faces looking down in their laps at glowing touchscreens. The show went less well than before and I haven't been asked back since.

In October of 2003 I drove onto Red Lake Indian Reservation in Minnesota for an assembly program at the high school. Because of widely publicized spree shootings, most notably Columbine High School, Red Lake installed an airport-style weapons detector at the front door. Schools were always full of locked doors, especially the theater (if they had one), and often my first task after checking in at the office was to find the janitor with his huge knot of keys to let me in where I needed to be. Here the entire school had become a medium security asylum. Two friendly security guards in street clothes were expecting me for my noon assembly. "It's okay," said one. "You can pass through. The machine isn't turned on." One of them escorted me to the gym which he unlocked so I could set up my sound system and arrange the chairs for hypnotic subjects.

While searching for the boy's lavatory I saw on the wall a notice that read: *HICKEYS WILL NOT BE TOLERATED.* Schools often drew battle lines over one thing or another: headwear, skirt length, printing on T-shirts. One school had a major issue over the π symbol appearing on walls and mirrors, which referred to some incident "too complicated to explain." As far as hickeys, they were common enough in high schools, but this was the first time I'd seen it as a disciplinary issue. The sign went on to read: *If you are seen with a hickey you will be sent to the office and it will be covered with makeup. If not, then you will be sent home.* In an isolated place like the Red Lake Reservation, what else was there for teenagers to do but suck each other's necks, especially knowing it was forbidden?

Rules against unconventional hairstyles had long since been abandoned in schools so I was used to every kind of coif, but nothing quite like the one on the hefty, alert-looking boy who passed me at the hickey sign. He had gelled it up into two spikes like horns. He was alone, I was alone. As one odd stranger to another we exchanged greetings and went our separate ways.

According to my usual show notes, I began my demonstration at 12:01 and ended at 1:13 p.m. I wrote that the audience was unfocused at first, but once the subjects (eight males and six females) were put into a trance and given suggestions of fishing, surf boarding, driving a monster bus, and eating ice cream cones, the audience responded wildly. After a few dismissals of those who came out of it, I ended with six male and three female subjects. On my personal scale of one to five I circled a five. For at least the hour I was there they forgot about hickeys and opened their minds to something else.

Less than a year and a half later I saw the horn-haired boy again, this time on TV and in the papers. He was identified as Jeff Weise, whose grandfather was a sergeant on the reservation police force. At 2:45 in the afternoon Weise, then sixteen, murdered his grandfather and another woman, stole his police car and crashed it into the front of the school. At the weapons detector (whether it was turned on or not didn't matter) he pulled out a semi-automatic pistol and shot one of the two friendly security guards. The other fled for his life. Weise proceeded to the left down the hall where I had first met him under the hickey sign, entered a classroom, and murdered seven more people. Then he put the pistol in his mouth and pulled the trigger. End of show.

Whether he was in "baseline consciousness" or a "trance state" during his murder spree is a matter of speculation. He was not among my subjects, but I assume he was in the audience. If he had decided to conduct his murder spree when I was hypnotizing his classmates in the gym, he would have had a greater concentration of potential victims, including myself. (Or, since I showed him a courtesy, he might have let me off, who knows.) Instead of the dubious distinction of pulling off the second largest high school shooting in American history (after

Columbine) he could have upstaged them and launched himself into first place. There's no question he would have upstaged me.

That's another school I have not been back to since.

Everyone wants to know, "Why?" They want answers. Simple ones, easy to understand. If we just do this. If we just do that. There is no lack of professional analysis and recommendation.

Psychologist David Walsh, leading proponent of "scripts" theory, proposes that certain behaviors (scripts) are "wired" into brains. Note his unintended comparison of suggested influence to electro magnetism by using the word "wired." Dr. George Realmuto, a University of Minnesota child psychiatrist, said on Public Radio that certain people are genetically predisposed to school shootings. "I don't think we have a mechanism for stopping them," he added.[1]

Clearly, a costly weapons detector did nothing to stop Jeff Weise. Addressing such issues as bullying and treating mental unbalance, factors in most if not all school shootings, is about all that can reasonably be done in addition to locking-up and buzzing-in. Dr. Edward Shorter, Faculty of Medicine at Toronto University, says, "It's hard to imagine an Adam Lanza [Sandy Hook massacre, twenty-eight dead] existing a century ago, before this culture of violence and depravity [was] available at *the click of a mouse or press of a button*" (emphasis added).

"Flashtunes" are user-friendly animations made with easily downloaded software. In August and September of 2004, a year before our brief meeting, Jeff Weise was deeply immersed in his private *baquet* of flashtunes on *Newgrounds.com*, a forum for videogamers. Many of the games were quite violent, like "Minute of Rage" ("Try to survive one minute in the deadly arena") and "Outsourced Hell" ("Manage your own little hell in this dark humored idle game"). Weise posted his own reviews of several games and amateur

---

1 Dan Olson, "Searching for Reasons Behind School Shootings," in Minnesota Public Radio website (March 23, 2005). news.minnesota.publicradio.org

animations, and, curiously, gave the highest rating to a notably nonviolent, minimalist piece titled "Hidden in the Snow," consisting of just one static image of three small, white, meteor-like streaks on a black background. We don't know whether Weise saw this image as a symbol of his own disintegrated family (he was the only child of an alcoholic mother and suicidal father), but his comment to the creator of this image was: "Jawohl... you've managed to captivate my simple, and often moronic, child-like, mind." He then added, "lacks three things: content, naked women, and guns..." The artist responded to Weise's comment by writing, "wth [what the hell] does jawohl mean?" All he had to do was Google the word and find it means the military "yes, sir" in German. Why German? Why did Weise identify himself elsewhere in a chat room as "Todesengel," German for "Angel of Death"? Why, as a Native American, did he idolize Hitler and become active on the website *Nazi.org*?

Weise posted two flashtune animations on *Newgrounds.com* under one of his various pseudonyms, one of them "Regret" (197 fans). The first was "Clown," a thirty-second feature beginning with a psychotic bozo trembling to a background of eerie death music by the goth band Evanescence. A male figure enters the frame and the clown grabs him. Cut to the clown's big shoes on which splats a huge gush of blood. The end.

"Target Practice" is another thirty-second feature by Regret with more complex animated movement. A male figure with no facial features except a horizontal bar across the eye area, appears carrying a bag. He coolly puffs a cigarette, removes an assault rifle from the bag and shoots four people, none of whom have faces either. One figure stands with hands behind its back as if a prisoner awaiting execution, another is simply a bystander, and another sits on a park bench. When the bullets hit, their heads explode in bursts of red. The shooter throws a hand grenade and blows up a police car before finishing off someone in a Klan hood. Then he puts a pistol in his mouth and pulls the trigger in a final blood-burst of red.

The similarities between "Target Practice" and Weise's March 21, 2005 performance at Red Lake High are so obvious they hardly need pointing out. It is a script for a mesmerizing stunt to be acted out before an audience. As of this writing, "Target Practice" is still posted on *Newgrounds.com* with over 500,000 views.

My role as stage hypnotist in schools allows me to hover like a drone over the impact crater of Weise's mass shooting. What I see is a show, a tragic one, with a stage left in disarray. Any performing hypnotist knows that adolescents are ideal subjects, and males get the best audience reaction. Progressive separation of their minds from reality occurs much faster and easier than with adults. School shooters like Weise and others experience prolonged separation from the world as they engross themselves in their digital *baquet* for hours and days and weeks on end, with no more mediating awareness of what they are doing than Mesmer's subjects in his Paris salon. Their fixation on their computers is an example of the imitative quality of staged influence that so concerned King Louis XVI's Royal Commission in 1784.

The Columbine shooters, Eric Harris and Dylan Klebold, victims of the ketchup squirt and other humiliations by jocks, retreated into their computers to such a degree the FBI report on their subsequent murder spree cited evidence taken almost entirely from the internet.[1] They convinced themselves they were Nazis in the same way that in 1881 E. B. Jennings, "Professor of Mesmerism," entertained a "ladies' sociable" at the Madison Avenue Congregational Church in New York, convinced one of their members that she dined with cannibals on "roast missionary" and said she "never tasted anything nicer."[2] This delusion was a gruesome, yet harmless, charade, but the deluded subjects at Columbine left fifteen dead, including themselves, plus twenty wounded, most among the computer terminals in the school library.[3] Hypnotic subjects, after their outlandish antics, often report no memory (post hypnotic amnesia) of what they did. Some remember only fragments. Others remember everything, fully aware of what they were doing, yet felt strangely compelled to do it. The level

---

1 hwebharvest.gov
2 *New York Times*, March 9, 1881.
3 "Eric Harris and Dylan Klebold," *Wikipedia* (wikipedia.org).

of consciousness of the Columbine killers at the time of their performance cannot be known. After all, there is no greater amnesia than death. What we do know for sure is that they touched the *baquet*. In fact, couldn't get loose from it.

Through the electro-mesmeric ether, the death show at Columbine traveled with the speed of thought to the mind of Jeff Weise, who copied it under the long shadow of the 1784 Commission warning of persons especially vulnerable to mesmeric influence. "The power wielded by the magnetizer over his patients is extraordinary," reads the Commission report. "...The *crises* [seizures] appear to be contagious [through a process of] mutual incitement and imitation... any public treatment where the means of Magnetism will be employed, can have in the long run only fatal effects."[1]

Spending more time at his computer than in the real world, Jeff Weise's mind began to channel the actions of Klebold and Harris. He imitated their wardrobe of the long black trench coat. Like them, he admired Hitler and planned his attack on the dictator's birthday. During the Columbine massacre Harris asked one of his victims before shooting her, "Do you believe in God?" Weise picked up the suggestion and parroted the same question before shooting one of his own victims.[2]

Ironically, Benjamin Franklin, who happened to be a member of the King's Commission investigating Mesmer, could not see the sinister effects of his own discoveries in electricity transmitting its own "fatal effects" over great distances. In Pennsylvania a parent found evidence in their child's internet chat group that they were planning a high school massacre on the 25th anniversary of the Columbine attack.[3] A seventeen-year-old in Winnenden, Germany murdered fifteen in apparent imitation of a similar rampage in Alabama that left eleven

---

1 *"émotion ... est augmentée par le spectacle d'émotions semblables...tout traitement public où les moyens du Magnétisme seront employés, ne peut avoir à la longue que des effets funestes."* Royal Commission Report, US National Archives website (search.archives.gov).
2 "Jeff Weise," *Mass-murder Fandom* (massmurder.fandom.com).
3 Victoria Albert, "Teens Charged with Planning Columbine-style attack at their High School" in *MSN News* [no date] (msn.com).

dead.[1] A teenager in Pennsylvania was jailed on suspicion of plotting a Columbine-style attack after exchanging e-mails with a student in Finland who killed eight people in a similar shooting.[2] They shared an interest in certain Web sites and online videos. A similar plot was uncovered in Cologne.[3] A school massacre in Erfurt exceeded the death toll at Columbine by two, with seventeen killed, including the shooter. According to the official Gutenberg Report on the Erfurt massacre, the nineteen-year-old perpetrator, Robert Steinhäuser, had in his room what are technically called "first person shooter games" (FPS) such as *Return to Castle Wolfenstein* and *Half-Life*, as well as the assassination game *Hitman; Codename 47.* Probably unawares, he missed Hitler's birthday by less than a week, landing instead on the birthday of William Shakespeare. As a bizarre coincidence, at the very moment of Jeff Weise's murder spree in Minnesota, a film on Shakespeare was being shown in a nearby classroom, which he overlooked because it was dark and so assumed the room was empty.

Criminologist Frank Robertz is quoted in the *Guardian:* "The phenomenon of massacres by young people in schools...has only existed since Columbine."[4] What Robertz understandably misses, probably because he's a criminologist and not a mesmerist, is that the seeds of Columbine itself began to germinate much earlier when the two magnetisms merged to massively inflate the imitative, unstoppable power warned about by King Louis XVI's Royal Commission. If nothing could be done about it then, what could be done about it now?

1 Carter Dougherty, "Teenage Gunman Kills 15 at School in Germany" in *New York Times,* March 11, 2009.
2 "Lawyer: U.S. Teen had no Warning of Finnish School Shooter's Plans," *CNN News.*
3 "Two Students in Germany Accused of Plotting a School Attack," wikinews.org.
4 "School massacre Plots Hatched on internet," *Mail & Guardian* (Nov. 21, 2007).

10 - You Call Me Violent I Kill You: Terror and Trance

The trick in all forms of influence, from getting someone to fantasize they're riding on a bus to actually blowing one up, is finding the right subject. A manipulator has to pick the right person(s), and cannot easily tell just by looking what degree they will respond. A test or tests, overt or disguised, are required to determine the subject's degree of suggestibility. I use the so-called "lock-out," or hand catalepsy method (copied from Edwin Baron) where the audience stands and clasps their hands together over their head. I say their hands are locking tighter and tighter and then I tell them they can't pull them apart. Most can, but the ones who can't are my choice as subjects. Without such a test, the operator is acting in the dark and dealing with unnecessarily high odds against success.

Hypnotic control is a manipulation of probabilities. There is no direct one-to-one causation of suggestion with response as commonly assumed, but rather a funneling of probabilities down to ever more predictable (but never certain) outcomes. For the stage hypnotist, if someone is willing to close their eyes and imagine a helium-filled balloon pulling up one hand—and the hand *actually rises*—they are more likely to see an elephant in a tree than those whose hand does not rise. Edwin Baron once told me with unusual honesty for a hypnotist, "I just play the percentages." There are other screening tests such as postural sway and inability to bend the arm or open the eyes, but whatever the indicative clue, it has to be there, or there is no next step. If a jihadist recruiter learns that someone already believes that blowing on their tea is a defiance of God's will, that's a reading on their level of suggestibility. It's a starting point. They are ready for the next step, then the next, and the next, hopefully ending with them pulling the pin in a bakery.

For an audience, of course.

The "terrorism" of al-Qaeda, Party of God, Tamil Tigers and others have the same goal of extreme action "intended," according to Title 22 of the U.S. Code Section 2656f(d), "to influence an audience." *The Art of Recruiting,* an Al-Qaeda manual compiled by Abu Amru Al Qa'idy, is essentially a hypnotism how-to book, presented as "a graded, practical program for recruiting via individual *da'wa* [influence]" through the latest electromagnetic technologies. "We will replace the (traditional) *halaqah* (seminar) with (modern) internet forums [i.e. the *baquet*]." Just as a hypnotist or *da'ee* (recruiter) cannot tell by looking at a person what degree they can be influenced, neither can anyone look within *oneself* to determine susceptibility either. In *Hypnotism Made Practical* (1943), J. Louis Orton states, "There are procedures that merely *lead up* to hypnosis...I propose to describe a few experiments from those I sometimes use in public demonstrations, whereby the induction of hypnosis may be facilitated." In the 1996 edition of *Encyclopedia of Stage Hypnotism* Ormond McGill writes, "Before you hypnotize anyone you wish to ascertain ... who among the group are the most susceptible..."

The al-Qaeda manual outlines a method for selecting subjects based on methods similar to those of Orton, McGill, myself and others. "You have to take him step by step," the *da'ee* advises. "Don't pass through one stage to another without achieving the goals of the previous stage..." Like the Stanford and Harvard scales of hypnotic susceptibility used in clinical applications, the manual grades the steps on a numbered scale. If the score is 19-24, "your choice was a good one ... your close relationship with him must continue." Like every hypnotist, al-Qaeda realizes there are those dream subjects with "the ability to change immediately." Finding them is a matter of statistical chance as well as patient method. Whether hypnotist or jihadist recruiter, both strive to bring their subjects to what Al Qa'idy calls "the Stage of Planting Concepts [Suggestions]." Once that point is reached, doubt and resistance have already been greatly reduced if not removed. Dr. Jerrold Post, Elliott School of International Affairs, George Washington University, asserts that terminal control is "not a quality of an individual but a property of a *relationship* [emphasis added] between a leader and ... followers," which sounds like James Randi's assertion that hypnotic influence is "merely an agreement between the subject and the operator that they will fantasize together."

Consent is modifiable up to and slightly beyond the point where one steps up on stage. After that, the spectacle moves by a sequence of manipulated probabilities toward the "life of its own," be it the Martian invasion, or the suitcase nuke. When the Great Maurice convinces a Las Vegas tourist to act like a duck, there's a good chance he will convince the same tourist to drop his pants for an even bigger laugh. Once the Ayatollah Khomeini uses the airwaves to plant the suggestion that Israel should be wiped off the map, it's a short step to persuading someone to mix up a glass of acetone peroxide on an airplane and wipe *themself* off the map, along with everyone else on board. It can't begin at the top of the suggestion pyramid. It must begin at the bottom.

French journalist Anna Erelle took on the assignment of pretending she was a jihadi subject online so she could write about their recruiting techniques. Her experience as "digital avatar" is described in her memoir, *In the Skin of a Jihadist* (2015). First, she found an appropriate chat room, then met a young terrorist named Bilel, who courted her as a potential wife (not telling her he was already married). In the name of research, she went along with it. Even though she knew she was acting, she found herself giving in to his persuasions. She was like the skeptical volunteer who goes up on stage intending to fake it and ends up as one of the best subjects. When their relationship went to video conferencing via Skype, she dressed the part by wearing a hijab. Under Bilel's influence she began to feel a "controlled schizophrenia." She could have used the word "trance" to describe her rational mind deteriorating under his Svengali-like spell. She "saw the impact of digital propaganda on God's newly minted soldiers." The expression "radicalized over the internet" could just as accurately be reworded to "mesmerized by the *baquet*." Her relationship with the jihadist recruiter ended when he discovered she had been faking as a subject, just as he had been faking as a suitor. Refractory subjects are bad enough, but outright saboteurs are intolerable. It ended with threats to her life and ongoing fear.

No one disagrees that contemporary terrorism is highly focused on electronic media, which is easy, cheap, and reaches millions. In 2009 Pentagon analysts testified before Congress that they monitored some five thousand jihadi websites. Terrorists, both foreign and domestic, enact their most lethal suggestions through the largest part of the Net, the so-called "Dark Web," a non-Googleable, non-traceable criminal haven comprising 87% of all websites, according to a lecture by computer forensic expert Mark Lanterman, former member of the U. S. Secret Service Electronic Crimes Taskforce. Combining this with layered encryption and steganography (concealed messages within another context) online terrorist activities are nearly impossible to detect. In a transcript of the 2011 Hearing Before the Subcommittee on Counterterrorism and Intelligence (no longer archived on the internet), William F. McCouts, Center for Naval Analysis, estimated that of all those who log on to jihadist websites, only .00001% end up as terrorists. He did not explain how he arrived at such a precise number, but his general point was that a wide reach will yield a small but effective number of recruits.

In 2014 the U.S. Government estimated only about a hundred Americans had joined jihadists in Syria, and a "few dozen" had joined ISIS. Those low numbers are more or less congruent with the missing 2011 Subcommittee on Counterterrorism transcript. Even though these percentages are much lower than the odds stage hypnotists have to deal with, they apply to a larger sampling and the results are still enough for the imitative effect to work.

In another missing report from 2015, the United Nations Security Council estimated that at least twenty-five thousand volunteers from one hundred foreign countries traveled internationally to join ISIS and al-Qaeda, proof of the efficacy of jihadi suggestions via the worldwide *baquet*. "Once alone in their bedrooms," the report stated, "[would-be terrorists] travel to their virtual world, which they take for reality." By 2017 the force size of Islamic State grew to an estimated tens of thousands to over two hundred thousand, but after their defeat in Iraq the numbers shrank to between 8,000 and 16,000. U.S.

officials indicated in early 2021 that the group was continuing to spread its ideology among vulnerable populations, some offering video games in which users as young as seven can pretend to be holy warriors killing U.S. soldiers.

Might we, like the radicalized screen watchers, be looking through the eyeholes of a collective chicken suit, thinking we are wide awake in the suggested fog of what we think is "reality"? Kafka saw this reality as a series of sliding paradoxes, where people perform mechanically from "a script that remains beyond their reach[1]." My interpretation, from years of experience in hypnotic staging, is that these scripts do not take us from reality to trance, but from trance to trance, like waking from one paradoxical dream only to slide into another. There will always be apostates, Luddites, contrarians, and non-cooperative subjects who wake up in mid-act and say, "it's not working," and find themselves kicked off the committee. But they will only go out and perform from another script.

Meanwhile, the indestructible *baquet* perpetuates itself in spite of its own paradoxes in the form of crashes, infowar, cyber-harassment, digital terrorism, cyber-break-ins and all manner of other dysfunctions. Until these dysfunctions should lead to the Net's complete self-annihilation, terrorist websites will continue to operate behind a wall of encryption and plant lethal suggestions in the minds of methodically selected subjects. It's a world the *baquet* has led us to. One can hear Mesmer's nemesis, the beheaded King Louis XVI, utter from the grave, "I told you so."

---

1 Carolin Duttlinger, *Kafka in Context* (2017) p. 97.

11 - The Anointed One Will Be with You Shortly

After I'm through inducing hypnotic subjects to do what they would "not ordinarily do," people frequently say, "Imagine what *governments* could do with that kind of power!" No need to imagine. It's already been done and is being done. Methods long established by dictators on the world stage bear an uncanny resemblance to the workings of hypnotists on their own stage. The goal in each case is to annihilate free will and rational thought, then give commands expected to be followed without question. And they are. Or else. Staging is all important. In both cases, those who "aren't working" are removed.

Perhaps the first observer to directly identify a dictator as hypnotist was George Bataille in his 1933 essay, "The Psychological Structure of Fascism," where he states that "the force of a [fascist] leader is analogous to that exerted in hypnosis." There is a "flow," as he called it, that unites dictator and followers with "violent and excessive energies that accumulate in the person of the leader." I have never been a dictator, but I have been a hypnotist and Bataille describes precisely what I do.

Hypnotists and tyrants do not usually wake up one morning and discover they have a unique power. They do not get a PhD in dictatorship, then go out and apply for the job. From beginning to end it's a function of will. Like all creatures, loathsome or otherwise, they evolve from simpler forms and follow more or less the same path to their respective niche. Hypnotists are known to begin as stage assistants, failed magicians, wedding DJs, birthday clowns. In my case it was professional plasma donor. They play the subservient role long enough to learn or steal the basics. Not all succeed. In fact, most do not, but the ones that do, anoint themselves "The World's

144

Greatest," "The Incredible," "The Amazing," "The Astounding" and so forth.

Had I not chosen the path I took, I might have had a conventional life rooted in a broadly familiar place, maybe with a teaching job somewhere following the proper orthodoxies. In my spare time I could have written poems on topics readers could relate to. Instead, I ended up in a life of terminal control. It's a lonely path. I began as the object of acceptance and rejection, then *I* was the one doing the accepting and rejecting. With increasing momentum, I acquired ever more power to turn people into gyrating, agitating, screaming laughingstocks. My feet no longer trod the same ground as my fellow human. It was something nature allowed to be done and I found a way to do it. I performed so many demonstrations in such tight sequence that they all became one demonstration, and my repertoire of manipulation became ever more refined. Even though I had the power to convince someone they had a rubber nose I could stretch all the way to the back of the room, it did not make me any more secure. It was all provisional and probabilistic, but I knew a thousand ways to jimmy the dice to roll the right numbers often enough.

The mileposts on this solitary path are servility, seizure, sovereignty. North Korea's Kim Il Sung began as such a weak-willed Sino-Soviet flunky that a Russian official once said, "We created him from zero."[1]

Idi Amin started his career of control by licking the fingers of his British military superiors who regarded him as a big, jolly, accordion-playing idiot. They realized they overestimated his subservience when he violently deposed fellow tyrant Milton Obote, then declared himself Conqueror of the British Empire in Africa and Lord of All the Beasts of the Earth and Fishes of the Seas. He eliminated a quarter-million people who did not dance to his tune, many of them fed live to crocodiles at Murchison Falls. Similarly, in Equatorial Guinea, Francisco Macías Nguema started as a corporate lackey controlled by the lawyer and wheeler-dealer, José Antonio García-Trevijano Fos, dean of the Faculty of Political Science

---

1 Marea Donnelly, "How Soviets' Kim Il-sung, Their Man in Korea, Went from 'Zero' to Family Dynastic Dictatorship" in *Daily Telegraph* (April 18, 2017).

and Economics at the University of Madrid. With perfect sycophancy Nguema rose in García-Trevijano's hierarchy.[1] When he was in a position to seize control, he did. Then he convinced a sufficient number of suggestible subjects that he could turn himself into a tiger and eat them if they did not follow his orders. As for the others, well, we know what happens to the others.

Pat Collins started off as a lounge singer of such meager promise that someone once made a cruel joke that she could be a hypnotist. Whether out of spite or luck, she did just that and went on to become hugely successful in Las Vegas and was featured in several TV specials where it was *her* making the cruel jokes, getting male subjects to crawl at her feet for laughs while she enticed them with one of her bad love songs. It worked so well that she had to hire a bodyguard who later told me his job was to protect her from jealous wives.

Dictators and hypnotists begin with a high likelihood of failure, which makes success all the more spectacular when it happens. Why else would Hitler call it *"my struggle"*? The riskiest part is the initial arrogation of power. That's why the beginning "induction," the part that has to take place before full control can be consolidated, is so perilous, yet so essential. It's why hypnotic induction scripts are sold on the internet as "foolproof" or "sure-fire," like maps to buried treasure. It's why wannabes secretly videotape the inductions of more successful hypnotists and copy them word for word. But will alone is not enough to bring about the magical results.

During the crucial induction phase, those who do not cooperate must be quickly eliminated, lest they counter-influence the others. If I see any of my subjects peeking or smirking, they are off the stage fast. When Saddam Hussein lined up stooges for his July 22, 1979 inauguration, sixty-six of them were escorted from the room. Then shot.[2] Is it a surprise that those remaining spontaneously rose to their feet and acclaimed him the undisputed "Anointed One, Glorious Leader, Direct Descendant of the Prophet, President of Iraq, Chairman

---

1 Randall Fegley, *Equatorial Guinea, An African Tragedy* (1989).
2 Con Coughlin, *Saddam, King of Terror* (2002) p. 158f.

of the Revolutionary Command Council, Field Marshall of its Armies, Doctor of its Laws, and Great Uncle to all its Peoples"? A bit much to fit on a business card, but if you're that anointed and glorious you don't need one.

With dictatorship, as well hypnotism, there is no allowance for failure. Many an unknown Hitler has flunked out and never was. I've seen novice hypnotists struggle and fail to get people "under" and leave the stage in utter humiliation. I know, I've been one. There is such a canyon of separation between the insignificant and the plenipotent that one wonders how it could ever be bridged by anyone. But for those who survive the early gauntlet of mistakes, there is a liminal event, a turning point where power rapidly inflates. People start slumping and falling off their chairs. They obey commands. A vortex of energy begins to swirl between the audience, and the one holding the mic. The exhilaration is indescribable. Next, it's the flashy suit, the gaudy rings, the Dali mustache.

Jean-Bédel Bokassa was a former bullied orphan and griddle cook from Bobangui, Central African Republic. When he pulled off a successful coup d'état he declared himself President for Life, Minister of Defense, Minister of Justice, Minister of Home Affairs, Minister of Agriculture, Minister of Health and Minister of Aviation. He bought a costume shop dictator's uniform, plastered it with over-the-counter medals, and on Napoleon's birthday threw a $22-million-dollar coronation for himself the country could not afford. He felt powerful enough to outlaw tom-toms and the bourgeoisie, and cultivated the practice of eating human flesh. It was said to be increasingly dangerous for anyone to contradict even slightly the crowned, bejeweled, ermine-draped, cannibal.[1] In 1939 Diana Spearman referred to this type of influence in *Modern Dictatorship*: "the concept of a man untrammelled by any restraints is curiously comforting to the human heart."

In a 2018 opinion piece in the *New York Times* titled "Donald Trump, Mesmerist," Professor Emily Ogden (University of Virginia) stated that "the more fetid the swamp of public life, the more important it [becomes] to understand the mesmeric

---

1 Alex Shoumatoff, *African Madness* (1988).

techniques of deception."[1] Two years later, in his memoir of serving as Trump's henchman, Michael Cohen mentions Mesmer by name in describing his boss's methods of total control and inducing denial in his subjects.[2] Tyrants from Hitler to Gaddafi, Putin to Bolsonaro, buoy themselves on masses of deceived supporters whose interests they care nothing about. It does not matter that the controllers make no sense, only that they cast the right "spells." Both the tyrant and the hypnotist act with intention and know instinctively what they want in the same way that a squirrel or a rat knows instinctively in a primal way what will further its interests. Subjects act less intentionally, and after the point of induction have no intention at all.

The Amazing Rudolph began as a playground wimp with high-water pants and a bad haircut. (I'm disguising his name because he directly competes with me in casinos and each of us would like nothing better than to see the other's head in a freezer.) He was easy to step on, both intentionally and by mistake. It's easy to understand how he would be drawn to hypnotic power and why he began following other hypnotists, including myself, around to performances. He figured out how to make people ride their chairs thinking they were jockeys at the Kentucky Derby, and walk through cow pies playing a tuba. He poached clients from the very people he stole his routines from, then hired telemarketers to sell him everywhere possible. The trajectory of his success was nearly vertical. Instead of going around hunched over and fearful of having his underwear yanked up, he started to swagger. He became cocky and obnoxious in his elevator shoes. With his ego in the stratosphere, he drove to gigs in a muscle car, his head barely rising above the steering wheel.

One night in Las Vegas I volunteered to be a participant in Justin Tranz's ninety-minute lounge show at Flamingo O'Shea's. I thought maybe I'd discover something I could use, just like Little Rudy faked his way up on the stage as one of my subjects at a county fair. As I followed his every command, I was

1 *New York Times*, August 4, 2018.
2 Michael Cohen, *Disloyal* (2020), p. 154. "[Trump's] getting otherwise seemingly sensible people to enter into his fantasyland...This is insanity up close and personal."

completely aware of what I was doing. I sang a rap song in Japanese and became the world's first pregnant man, giving birth to a monkey. People were not laughing *with* me; they were laughing *at* me. I suppose I could have walked away at any time, but I did not. Like Uday Hussein's body double, "The longer I served the dictator, the more removed from reality I became."[1] I would describe my "trance" in the words of someone quoted in *I Was Saddam's Son* (2013): "I just stepped into that painfully bright white space in my brain that had the power to burn away [critical thought] like overexposed film." Even though I did not think I was "under," I was conscious of Mr. Tranz monitoring me a thousand times a second. I wasn't worried about him drilling my body with a power tool, but the idea of getting up and leaving was out of the question.

As the vortex of absolute control swirls into its final flush, simple convincingness is no longer enough for the Anointed One. Total soul-rooted devotion becomes the absolute requirement, and even that isn't enough. Mussolini was so aware of the subversive power of uncertainty that he made it illegal for newspaper headlines to print question marks.[2] I've heard of hypnotists whispering violent off-mic threats to subjects not reacting properly. I can't even begin to imagine what would happen to a subject with the audacity to openly defy the Great Maurice. I had a nightmare once where I maniacally clubbed a resisting subject with my microphone, like President Jean-Bédel Bokassa used his cane to beat to death six kids who threw rocks at his exalted motorcade.[3] Upon awakening, I was disturbed, very disturbed, that I was capable of such a dream. It's what extreme control can do to a person.

Dr. Castillo Gonzales, a linguist and expert on the Fang philosophical vocabulary in Equatorial Guinea, was thought by President Francisco Macías Nguema to be insufficiently convincing in his performance as a presumed subject. He was arrested and thrown in prison where he died. The "President for Life" ordered Dr. Gonzales's head opened to see if there was

---

1 Latif Yahia, *I Was Saddam's Son* (1997), p. 92.
2 Ruth Ben-Ghiat, *Strongmen, Mussolini to the Present* (2020), p. 101.
3 *African Madness,* cited above, p. 117. Too exhausted to finish the job, President Bokassa had associates do the same thing to the remaining 143 classmates, by far the largest school massacre in world history.

anything inside it to indicate what made him so undeceivable. Finding nothing of out of the ordinary, Professor Gonzales' gray matter was put to a more practical use. It was eaten by his captors.[1]

It should not be surprising that hypnotists and dictators are influenced by their own ballyhoo, since they are the only ones who have ever been present at each and every one of their performances. Add to this the absolute isolation that goes with absolute control. What self-awareness could be expected from someone forced to live a life of decoy motorcades, body doubles, disguises and paranoiac nights in more beds than could possibly be kept track of? How often would they wake up (as I do in endless motels) with no idea where they are? All they have to cling to is their hold on power, which is provisional and probabilistic, and always on the verge of slipping away. And slip away it often does, accompanied by ludicrous denials. When Serbian President Slobodan Milošević was transferred to the Hague Tribunal to face charges of genocide (100,000 deaths), his wife Mirjana—who controlled him like a puppeteer—told a reporter, "Prison? In fact, I wonder why my husband is there." She thought the whole genocide thing would go away and she would be in Lugano, Switzerland wearing a white dress and a flower in her hair, eating ice cream with hubby. [2]

After Idi Amin was deposed and the Tanzanian Army had invaded the country, he made several broadcasts claiming he was in Kampala and still in control, even though station employees deny that he had been there. Various sources speculate he used mobile transmitters fitted into several of his cars.[3] When Ethiopia's President Mengistu Haile Mariam was imprisoned for murdering 500,000 uncooperative subjects, he denied he was in prison at all.[4] When French Legionnaires moved into Central African Republic to depose Jean-Bédel Bokassa (raised by Catholic missionaries), they found him

---

1 *Equatorial Guinea, An African Tragedy*, cited above, p. 80.
2 Dragan Bisenic, "The Sound and the Fury of Mirjana Markovic" in *Ha'aretz Magazine* (Aug. 15, 2001).
3 Martha Honey, "The Fall of Idi Amin: Man on the Run" in *Washington Post* (April 14, 1979).
4 Riccardo Orizio, *Talk of the Devil, Encounters with Seven Dictators* (2002), p. 155.

ready to chow down on the cadavers of student protesters kept in large freezers in his lavish home. He must have found it devastating that no one believed him when he said he was "secretly named by the Pope as 13th apostle of the Holy Mother Church."[1]

The rare dictator ends his days in pampered self-delusion, like Idi Amin living among oil sheikhs in an exclusive area of Jedda on a generous monthly stipend from the Saudi government, driving his choice that day of a white Cadillac or a Maserati. It was reported that he liked to turn his face upwards whenever he said the name of God, which was often.[2]

But for others their show closes with prison, murder, execution, suicide. Saddam Hussein may or may not have had a flash of insight the moment his neck snapped as he dropped through the trap door, or Mu'ammar Al-Qadhdhāfī when pulled from a sewer pipe, or Slobodan Milošević at the instant his heart gave out in his war crimes detention cell at The Hague. It's more likely they remained delusional to the very end.

Aging dictators, like aging mesmerists, exercise diminishing energy and influence trying to hold absolute control. Ben Vandermeide ("Europe's Fastest Hypnotist"), once king of kings in the state fair market, ended his days haunting the International Fairs and Expo Convention in Las Vegas, trying to get a new generation of controllers involved in some secret booking scheme. They all ignored him. Previous admirers and trusted allies are often the likeliest to usurp control. Many a tyrant has been snuffed by a confidante. Many a hypnotist has seen the act filched by a friend, assistant, lover.

Then the cycle begins anew.

---

1 William Underhill, "Lives of the Dictators," in *Newsweek* (March 16, 2003).
2 Yunusu Abbey, "An Audience with Big Daddy Idi" in *The New Vision* (Kampala), reprinted in *The Mail & Guardian* (Feb., 1999).

12 - Trump and the Q Trick

The authoritarian controller, on whatever stage, gives "life" to what does not exist. What *does* exist is the desperate urge for that life to continue. In the May 27, 1939 edition of the family-oriented *Saturday Evening Post* was an article titled "Star-Spangled Fascists." It stated that "fascism in America continues to prosper and spread." The German-American Bund, a branch of the Nazi party in Germany, had chapters across America with membership upwards of 200,000 and published four newspapers as well as a magazine for youth. Pelley Publishers produced a daily and weekly magazine for Nazi sympathizers as well as 30,000 pieces of hate literature per day. The *Post* article estimated the number of speeches by fascist leaders as "near astronomical." Its vast Norman Rockwell readership was already familiar with Father Charles Coughlin's anti-Semitic radio broadcasts and the sermons of Reverend Gerald Winrod, an ardent fan of Hitler. Other names well-known at the time were George Deatherage, distributor of English language white supremacist material published in Germany, and Major General George Van Horn Moseley, the Nazi-booster who addressed an audience of 20,000 in Madison Square Garden. A third of all the families in America, the *Post* stated, received Nazi literature with some degree of regularity.

Despite the widespread phenomenon of hate mixed with patriotism, the article noted that no charismatic leader had yet come forward in America to unite all the extreme factions as Hitler had done in Germany. Of the numerous Reverends, Generals and Grand Wizards going about pontificating Aryan superiority, none had trumped all the others. Not yet. The article went on to say, "The horse is still riderless... The Leader, when or if he comes, will have something to lead."

Having something to lead (subjects) and actually leading (performing the act) are two separate components that need a catalyst—timing. Circumstances have to be historically opportune. In 60 AD a Roman mathematician named Heron of Alexandria invented the first steam engine which could have been used to power a vehicle at a time when there was no screaming need.[1] Horses and slaves were considered sufficient until history was ready for the traffic jam. Although TV had been around for decades, it took the prosperous 1950s for it to become commonplace. Anti-Semitic militarism suppurated in fin de siècle Europe before WWI, spreading by the slow means of printed words and shouted speech, but came alive with the invention of radio and amplified sound.

As a thought experiment, I've imagined myself lining up subjects in chairs for a hypnosis demonstration at, let's say, a fair in the Middle Ages. How successful would I be in getting subjects to fall into a trance and see a flower growing out of my head? Would they have even the slightest idea what I was trying to do? Most likely they would slot me into the next closest thing familiar to them, probably something demonic. That's exactly what happened when I did my act in remote places in Mexico and the West Indies where they had never heard of hypnotism. Reactions weren't what I hoped. No one went into a trance. I was not entertaining. There was no applause. They saw me as a nut practicing some perverted black magic and their response was the urge to eliminate me, more or less literally, much to the concern of my handlers, not to mention myself.

In 1939 the horse of fascism was still riderless in America as the *Post* stated, but a short century later on the internet and right-wing radio, there appeared a hypnotic delusion known as Q, a non-existent crypto-person. Who is Q? *Where* is Q? Precisely. Some believe (via the Net of course) that Q is Austin Ryan Steinbart, an actual convicted hacker-extortionist[2] cum walking hypnotic subject, who claims to be

---

1 Animated reconstruction on *YouTube*: youtube.com/watch?v=BG85rdGng7g.
2 Department of Justice, U.S. Attorney's Office, District of Arizona.

living in the future and posting messages backward in time by means of quantum computing.[1]

The internet has made Q into a matrix of paranoias more or less stemming from the core delusion that the world is run by a secret cabal of child-trafficking extra-terrestrials associated with anything pertaining to humanist values. It's the equivalent of losing control of yourself in Mesmer's salon. In its nebulous personification, Q speaks the "Real Truth," laughable as it is, from a hidden place deep inside the government and disseminated to millions on the Net, which could not have happened at any time other than the present. What before would have attracted at best a few hecklers to a soapbox spieler, can now influence and control millions in seventy countries. In 2020 the London-based Institute for Strategic Dialogue, which tracks disinformation around the world, chronicled a five-month tripling of Q Web interactions from 2.35 million to 7.26 million[2].

Q encourages their internet followers to put random absurdities together and create their own illusions. In Japan, for example, those influenced by Q have come up with the idea that the royal family consists of body doubles, and the bombings of Hiroshima and Nagasaki were fake.[3] Stage hypnotist Edwin Baron, without making direct suggestions but only subtle questions and gestures, would observe the slightest spontaneous behavior from a subject and then call attention to it until the behavior ballooned out of control. It looked like he was somehow the cause, when in fact it was autosuggestion. "I see your leg is shaking ... look, it's shaking more ... now it's shaking out of control ... why can't you stop?" In a matter of seconds, the subject becomes a spasmic, leg-shaking wreck before a laughing audience.

When I see footage of people at Q rallies jumping to their feet and pulling at Q messages on their T-shirts, they look *exactly* like hypnotic subjects screaming "The British are coming!" or "I wet my pants!" Q runs podcasts that mimic news programs and Google takes them down at a rate just short of

---

1 rationalwiki.org/wiki/Austin_Steinbart.

2 Nathan Bomey and Jessica Guynn, "How QAnon and Other Dark Forces are Radicalizing Americans" in *USA Today* (Aug. 31, 2020, updated Oct. 2, 2020).

3 Alex Silverman, "QAnon Is Alive and Well in Japan" in *The Diplomat* (Jan. 29, 2021).

that at which Q put up new ones. A Google search will turn up 9 to 13 million Q sites, depending on the browser, all with different names. On the encrypted messaging app *Telegram*, someone called GhostEzra tells more than 300,000 followers that President Biden is dead and has been replaced by an actor wearing a rubber mask, a claim promoted by Lin Wood, aspiring to be the next Republican Party chairman in South Carolina.[1]

In Kentucky and Colorado, mothers mesmerized by Q websites kidnapped their own children, deluded into thinking they were targeted by a child trafficking ring.[2]

In Waco, Texas, a woman influenced by the Q conspiracy crashed into two cars she was chasing, because, she said, she was "saving a child from pedophiles."[3] In 2016, Edgar Maddison Welch fired an AR-15 assault rifle into the Comet Ping Pong Pizza Parlor in Washington DC because he thought it was a Democrat-run sex slavery ring.[4]

Soon, other pizza parlors, cafes, bookstores, and bistros were attacked, as well as musicians who performed in them.

An FBI intelligence bulletin warns that "these conspiracy theories very likely will emerge, spread, and evolve in the modern information marketplace, occasionally driving both groups and individual extremists to carry out criminal or violent acts."[5] Haven't we heard this before from King Louis XVI's Royal Commission on mesmerism and its exploitation of the "involuntary instinct of imitation"?

Many of the rioters that stormed the US Capitol on January 26, 2021, where four people died, waved Q banners and signs, and wore Q hats and T-shirts. They were all "red-pilled," latter-day fascist slang for "awakened."

---

1 Ewan Palmer, "Lin Wood Shares Post Claiming Joe Biden is Dead, Trump Still in White House" in *Newsweek* (April 30, 2021).

2 Will Sommer, "QAnon Mom Charged with Kidnapping Her Kids" in *Daily Beast* (Mar. 28, 2020). Elisha Fieldstadt, "Colorado woman, inspired by QAnon conspiracy, sought to kidnap her own child" in *NBC News* (Jan. 7, 2020).

3 Snejana Farberov, "QAnon supporter...charged" in *Dailymail* (Aug. 21, 2020).

4 "Gunman in 'Pizzagate' Shooting is Sentenced to 4 Years in Prison," Maathew Hoog and Maya Salem, *New York Times* (July 22, 2017).

5 Yaron Steinbuch, "FBI: Conspiracy theory 'extremists' are a terror threat" in *New York Post* (Aug. 1, 2019).

Or said another way, "put under" by the long-awaited leader on the horse of fascism.

White-haired, retired engineer William Tapley, who wears a crucifix around his neck and calls himself the "Third Eagle of the Apocalypse," is a Q believer. "When [Trump] takes down the deep state," he says on one of his podcasts (since taken down by YouTube), "there could be bloodshed." Who but Tapley, *soi-disant* expert on phallus symbols at the Denver International Airport as well as everywhere around us, could be qualified to proclaim that the real identity of Q is—Donald J. Trump![1]

A spokesperson on the Anti-Defamation League website advises that people have an obligation to tell Q believers they are deluded and provide evidence to show why. I can't disagree with that advice, but I know from long experience that hypnotic suggestions cannot be neutralized by reason. It's even the basis of my funniest stunts. I can tell a hypnotic subject his nose is made of rubber, then ask someone from the audience to step up and tell him that it is *not* made of rubber. "*Go ahead, feel it.*" In spite of evidence to the contrary, the subject is still bound to my suggestion. I can proceed to grasp the subject's "rubber" nose and stretch it all the way to the back of the room then turn loose, whereupon his head snaps back and knocks him out of his chair.

What allows a controller such as myself—or Trump—to get on that horse and ride high in the saddle is having the means to pull it off at the right time. Congressman Gregory Meeks of New York told CNN News that Trump has "the biggest megaphone in the world," that is, the amplified power of digital media.[2] He is at the right time in history and with the right means to make repeated suggestions to those most susceptible.

In his 2020 biography of Idi Amin, Mark Leopold noted that the Ugandan dictator was years ahead of Trump in using inane behavior to manipulate populist support. Amin may have

---

1 Anderson Cooper, *CNN* (June 17, 2011).
2 Tim Hanes, "Rep. Gregory Meeks: Trump Has the Biggest Megaphone in The World, But Chooses Not to Condemn White Supremacy" in *Real Clear Politics* website (Mar. 19, 2019).

acted the fool on the world stage by putting tabasco in the drink of his own general, Moses Ali, or sending a telegram to Queen Elizabeth, inviting himself to Britain at her expense. Mass media at the time put him on the high horse of power to his base in and out of Uganda (including the US). With more pervasive mass media, Trump has parlayed similar idiocy that windmills cause ear cancer,[1] alligator moats should be built along the Mexican border,[2] and George Washington "took over airports" during the Revolutionary War.[3] The results are obviously impressive. I too stay with what works.

In the game of control, bad outcomes are always possible. But as long as the controller stays on stage (in office) the bad outcomes can be denied. However, when the show is over, so is control as well as denial of its failure. When authoritarians leave office, vulnerability increases. Trump was not the only authoritarian desperate to hold onto power as the end neared. In the jargon of international relations, it's "gambling for resurrection," which means the employment of diversions to deflect attention from the mess you're in. When failing to hypnotize anyone, hypnotists often resort to the resurrection gamble as a last diversionary resort before grabbing their money and rushing out the back. I once saw a hypnotist, after an awful barroom failure, do the old sideshow stunt of pounding a railroad spike up his nose. I wouldn't say it saved him, but it got him off better than otherwise.

To distract from accusations of collaborating with Russia in interfering with the 2016 presidential election, Trump ordered air strikes against Syria, and in the midst of his first impeachment he staged a drone hit on Iran's General Qasem Soleimani. When he failed to get reelected, he manipulated Q supporters and their allies to seize the nation's Capital, which not only took attention off his failures, but strengthened support within his base.

After a less than triumphant show in my early phase of learning hypnotism, a woman came up to me and said, "So you're a little Hitler. Is that what you want to be?" I couldn't

---

1 abcnews.com
2 meaww.com
3 latimes.com

really say yes, and I couldn't really say no, so I stammered something incoherent which only emphasized her point. I hadn't yet learned, like Trump, to deny, deny, deny the reality of my failures.

13 - Listen Only to My Voice: Cults

Hypnotists often acquire what people call a "cult following." At some venues they perform for weeks and months at a time, like Dr. Michael Dean at the Gaslight Supper Club in San Diego. I've had subjects return night after night to my own performances, even follow me to other towns, so addictive is the need of certain people to be controlled. Cult leaders exploit this tendency—as I do—by persuading their subjects to believe the nonsensical. Some are even hypnotists, like the charlatan Georgei Gurdjieff, who claimed to cure drug addicts through hypnosis,[1] or Nancy Salzman, the hypnotherapist and co-founder of NXIVM, famous for branding female sex slaves like cattle.[2] The carefully staged selection, induction, and reinforcement methods of cult leaders are similar to mine. The difference is, I eventually wake my subjects up and they don't.

So peculiar is this human tendency to be controlled, that people will give the last penny of their inheritance to a bearded fraud with ninety-three Rolls-Royces.[3] No appeal to reason will change their mind. I can bring someone up from the audience to try and convince a hypnotized subject they are not really milking an imaginary cow, but they will keep milking. Years of news reports and documentaries have exposed the cannibalization of people's lives by cults, yet people keep joining. Over 3,000 cults operate with impunity within the US

---

1 Anthony Storr, *Feet of Clay, Saints, Sinners and Madmen: A Study of Gurus* (1996), p. 24.

2 Sarah Berman, *Don't Call it a Cult, The Shocking Story of Keith Reniere and the Women of NXIVM* (2021), pp. xiii, 24.

3 *Wild Wild Country*, Netflix documentary (2018) and summarized in *The Irish Sun* (March 22, 2018).

alone.[1] No country is exempt. They thrive like mold on month-old bread.

In the course of my stage career, I've encountered all types of cultists, from Moonies to Scientologists, followers of Bhagwan Rajneesh and disciples of televangelists and faith healers. Sometimes they are subjects, sometimes not. They take me aside for private talk or write me letters with the similar theme of telling me that I am on the wrong path and they can help me find the right one. Like addicts who switch from one addiction to another, they might belong to the Children of God one year, Hare Krishna the next, then move on to the Landmark Forum. Something draws them to my show.

Cults are religions, however perverted, and religions are cults, however benign. Both are systems of control. In *Varieties of Religious Experience* (1917) William James reduced religions down to two essential elements: a problem (something wrong) and a solution (redemption).[2] Cultists who approach me unbidden have a deep-seated sense of something wrong. They are either searching for—or are certain they have found—redemption. They have an underlying fear that what redeems them may in fact be a lie, and so they have a great need to ratify what they believe.

In 1915 Emile Durkheim drew a line of continuity from the role of "sacred beings" in primitive cultures to "cult" leaders in modern society.[3] The preacher, guru, hypnotist, represents a "break in continuity" between the "profane" (William James's "problem") and the "sacred" (James's "redemption"). The cult leader *must* declare the two realms incompatible. If they begin to mix, the sacred evaporates. That's why cults obsessively sequester their members with all manner of interdicts, the violation of which brings swift and harsh judgement, like Jim Jones of Peoples Temple (remember the cyanide Kool Aid?) who had people beaten in front of his congregation if they profaned his holiness in even the slightest way.[4] Bhagwan Rajneesh, the Rolls-Royce cultist, turned his followers into sex

---

1 Steven Hassan, *Combating Cult Mind Control* (2016), p. 81.
2 Lectures VI and VII. "The Sick Soul."
3 *The Elementary Forms of the Religious Life,* Book 3, "The Principal Ritual Attitudes."
4 *San Francisco Chronicle,* June 16, 1978, p. 2.

objects, some of whom laid out poison for the inhabitants of an entire town because they challenged his almightiness.[1]

There are many conscious states and we cannot be in all of them at once. Many are in direct opposition (e.g., faith / doubt). If a controller directs someone by careful steps to one particular conscious state, it will expand at the expense of the other(s). And the other(s) must be obliterated at all cost.

A system of suggestive control does not have the fixed dimensional boundaries of an object, like a monocle or top hat. It doesn't begin here and end there. It can spread to infinity in all directions. Durkheim observed that religious force has a way of extending itself in a process he termed "contagiousness" to establish its "empire" over converts and co-religionists[2].

There was a time when concerned family members paid professional brain-washers to kidnap their ensnared loved ones, take them to a place outside their "empire," and harangue them for days until the "wrong" conscious state broke down and they were back to "normal." As cults have become more refined, according to ex-Moonie and anti-cult crusader Steven Hassan, so have the deprogrammers. It's a hypnosis show in reverse, where someone in the audience takes over from the hypnotist and tries to undo their suggestions. *The cow is not there, so stop milking it!* Compared to my hour of strutting upon the stage, cults work their act for months or years, and neutralizing their suggestions is neither easy nor always successful. The more refined "Strategic Interactive Approach," pioneered by Hassan, aims to reposition, by gentle suggestion, the subject's identity from a place of denying they are in a cult, to accepting that they are, and finally replacing that identity with a new one.[3] No cult member is going to say, "Look, I'm in a cult!" But that's the first admission the deprogrammer will want the subject to make. We must bear in mind, however, that there are vastly more cults than deprogrammers.

---

1 *Wild Country* Netflix documentary series cited above.
2 Durkheim, cited above, p. 360.
3 *Combating Cult Mind Control,* cited above, p. 202.

When is a cult not a cult? We don't question the definition applying to NXIVM, Heaven's Gate, or People's Church, but what about Tupperware, the Boy Scouts, Daughters of the American Revolution, or for that matter academic departments at universities? What about sports teams, ethnic identity, fashion? Thomas Merton talks of postulants entering the monastic order "stripped of an old ideology and clothed with a new one," which he calls "the absolute rightness of what we have always accepted."[1] This paradox is presented in practical terms by Anthony Storr in his insightful study of cults, *Feet of Clay* (1996): "Idiosyncratic belief systems which are shared by only a few... are likely to be regarded as delusional. Belief systems which may be just as irrational but which are shared by millions are called world religions."[2]

It's a paradox that has been around a long time. In the 4th century BC, Eubuludes of Miletus suggested picturing a heap of sand. How many grains, he asked, do you need to take away before you reach a point where you no longer have a "heap"?

Similarly, how many delusional systems do you have to abandon before you realize you are not in one?

---

1 Thomas Merton, *Monastic Journey* (1977), pp. 121-122.
2 p. 203.

14 - A Note on Proof

In 2005 Dr. Amir Raz brought a clinical hypnotist into his laboratory at Cornell University to hypnotize eight subjects. They didn't just sit in a slump. As in my show, they had to *prove* they were under, and to do that they were required to perform. Do what they wouldn't ordinarily do. But in this case, it was not especially crowd-pleasing. Their stunt was what neurologists call the Stroop effect, where someone identifies the colors of printed words printed in a different color. For example, the word BLUE might be printed in RED letters. It takes effort. The Cornell subjects were given the post-hypnotic suggestion that the word they saw had no meaning, only gibberish. The intended effect was to make it easier to identify the color and thus neutralize the Stroop effect.

Raz already knew that when an area of the brain is in use, blood flow to that region increases, and this increase is linked to neural activity, which can be measured. When someone struggles with the Stroop problem, an area of the brain called the anterior cingulate cortex (ACC) always lights up. If a person is given the post-hypnotic suggestion that the Stroop word is no longer a word but nonsense letters, the color should be easier to identify and the ACC would be inactive.

To measure this lack of activity in the ASC, Raz needed a prop, in this case a 3.0-tesla General Electric functional magnetic resonance imaging machine (fMRI). Fortunately, his affiliation with Cornell gave him access to this $300 thousand-dollar prop, as well as people who knew how to run it. With wires sprouting out of their skulls, his subjects—with their post-hypnotic suggestion—sat in front of a computer screen and proceeded to identify Stroop colors while a technician read their ACC levels on the fMRI. As expected, the hypnotized subjects showed no ACC activity when reading the color-word scramble. A non-hypnotized control group lit up like a Christmas tree. When Raz published his results in *Proceedings of the National Academy of Science*[1], the popular media seized upon it as scientific proof at last that there was such a thing as the hypnotic state.

Raz's experimental model was air-tight, but conclusions in the press were somewhat less so. His experiment did establish that ACC activity in the brains of select people was affected by suggestion. It did *not* directly prove the existence of a state of consciousness commonly referred to as "hypnotic trance."

Without disputing Raz's results, there is one component of his experimental design that someone like myself would notice. He describes with great precision the brain activity of his subjects ("T2*-weighted gradient echo planar imaging sequence with an in-plane resolution of 3.44 X 3.44 millimeters sampled at 250 Hz with 128-electrode dense-array geodesic sensor net referenced to the vertex"). But the *hypnotist* is not even mentioned by name, in fact, not even mentioned at all. Who is (s)he? If there is video footage (as there is for Skinner's Ping-Pong pigeons) of the selection and induction of subjects, I have not been able to find it. All we know is, an unidentified someone staged a "hypnotic episode" using "a standard hypnotic induction," apparently from a script available on the internet. Selection of subjects followed the one-at-a-time thirteen-step Stanford Hypnotic Suggestibility Scale (Form C), also available verbatim on the internet, with its tedious "if-this-go-to-that" formula.[2] A subject following such tedium might show an attentional predisposition that itself could influence the Stroop effect.[3]

It has been a stereotypical assumption that hypnotists, clinical or theatrical, are generic practitioners with

---

1 Amir Raz, Jin Fan, and Michael I. Posner, "Hypnotic Suggestion Reduces Conflict in the Human Brain," in *Proceedings of the National Academy of Science* (July 12, 2005), Vol. 102, no. 28, p. 9978-9983.

2 leevonk.com

3 Raz notes this possibility and cites three studies that challenge the robustness of the Stroop effect. *Proceedings of the National Academy of Science*, cited above, p. 9978.

interchangeable skills of equal competency. In reality, they range from persuasive virtuosos down to inarticulate bunglers. In clinical seminars I've seen hypnotic techniques by licensed therapists with no elocutionary skills (not to mention execrable wardrobe and oral hygiene) uncritically accepted by a closed audience of sympathetic peers. It's also possible that someone with rare talent can zero in on perfect subjects with rapid speed and perform spectacular results. Yet even then, how do we know for certain anyone is *really* in a hypnotic state?

Nonetheless, the Raz study proves that suggestion, in at least one delimited situation, can work its way into the deepest part of the human brain and solder itself onto its hard wiring.

Conclusion

Can you resist hypnotic control?

The question should include influence in general. In her long-forgotten memoir, *Autobiography of an Actress* (1854), Anna Cora Mowatt describes her experience of being in the presence of a mesmerist. "The room filled with a dim haziness and objects began to dance and float, and then disappear." If we share anything universally, it's an innate susceptibility to suggestion in some way or another, and we have no more control over it than the color of our eyes. Socrates regarded self-examination as the key to negating delusion, but we all know that keys can be notoriously sticky and sometimes not work at all. I encounter people all the time who are aware of a suggestive propensity in themselves and absolutely refuse to be hypnotized on stage. They may leave the room entirely or, in spite of themselves, begin reacting to suggestions from their seat in the audience, causing a distraction, and end up on stage after all.

When he was alive, Edwin Baron performed the stunt where he asked a subject, apparently wide awake and not in a trance, "Do you think you're hypnotized?" The answer was usually no. Then he said, "If that's the case, why have you forgotten your name?" whereupon the subject would wrinkle their brows with great concern at the blank where their name used to be.

Ask yourself the same question: do you feel hypnotized? The answer is probably no because you "know everything that's going on." What you are not aware of is that "everything that's going on" is the very suggestion you are acting out, the cumulative result of a lifetime of influence that has been staged. Your awareness of "everything that's going on" would be totally different if you were, let's say, a Sindhi-speaking nomad of Tharparkar. You would still think you were "awake" and know "everything that's going on," yet in a completely different reality. So, who's awake and who's in the trance?

One might argue that in spite of our individual and cultural differences our minds all work the same way, and the range of perceived reality is relatively narrow. Wouldn't everyone everywhere agree that a rock is a rock? The German philosopher Edmund Husserl used the term *lebensvelt* (a word without an exact equivalent in English) to describe a universal agreement on supposedly simple, obvious things, like a rock. But even this simple perception would have little similarity to how a rock is perceived, for example, by a person of Hanga Atoll, who spends a lifetime moving a human-sized stone around the island for deep-seated cultural reasons, and if they drop it, it means they must die.[1] A large percentage of present-day Icelanders, arguably the most educated people in the world, believe that invisible people live under and around stones everywhere, and road construction and housing plans are altered to avoid disturbing them.[2] Imagine what shared reality there would have been between an 18th century Jesuit missionary and a Jivaroan headshrinker in the Amazon persuaded to convert to the Church of Rome. Further imagine what would—and did—happen to the padre's head and the unshared perceptions it contained.[3]

The Yanomamö Indians in Venezuela have been described as the most violent people in the world, right up there with the Jivaro. According to anthropologist Napoleon Chagnon (1938-2019) who lived with them for eleven years, they have no concept of natural death, since virtually everyone dies by homicide sooner or later. A few tribesmen confided to him that some of their beliefs are ridiculous, a perception they could never share within their culture.[4] If they had any sense, that is.

1 Paul Theroux, *Fresh Air Fiend* (2000), "Unspeakable Rituals and Outlandish Beliefs." Also cited in Chapter 1.

2 businessinsider.com.

3 See *Ultimate Potential New Civilizations Review* (May, 2022).

4 Phone interview, 2004. Chagnon himself has been involved in vicious academic controversies sometimes bordering on violence, according to one of his colleagues, Dr. Wayne Allen. (Private conversation.)

Granted, with the ubiquity of mass (and "social") media in places where electromagnetism has found its way, there may be the appearance of congruent reality across borders. How deep the congruence is another matter. But if human perception actually did overlap more than at the peripheries, there would be no bad neighborhoods, no culture wars, no ethnic cleansing, or clash of civilizations. To the long list add serial killers and their many, many fans. For better or worse, we are all lost in a trance. But, alas, not the same one.

On its chosen platform, staged influence moves people toward automatic behavior, sometimes good, sometimes bad. One can only rely on self-examination and critical thinking to balance the more ludic aspects of this influence, but we have to expect limited effect from reason alone. There are those who will deny on stage their leg is shaking out of control just as there are those who will deny there is a pandemic as they lie dying from it. George Steiner pointed out the "bleak paradox" that the humanities and the inhuman can be intimately connected, where someone can read Goethe in the evening and go to work at Auschwitz in the morning.[1] Even paragons of insight can be as vulnerable to suggestive influence as any hypnotic subject exhibited to the public. Martin Heidegger, considered one of most important philosophers of the twentieth century, imagined himself the philosophical eminence of the Third Reich. Hannah Arendt, Jewish historian and author of *Eichmann in Jerusalem* (1963) and *The Origins of Totalitarianism* (1951), fell romantically (and vice versa) for the much older Professor Heidegger. Ezra Pound, architect of modernist poetry, was magnetized by Mussolini and made radio broadcasts on his behalf ("I lost my center..."). Jean-Paul Sartre, Nobel Prize notwithstanding, fell for Stalin.

The mirrored hall of staged reality can have its rooms of suggested benevolence. Organized religion may counterbalance the more wicked suggestions of those in a position to make them (which often enough are those within the religion itself). There's the sublimity of art. It's hard to say that animal magnetism's Siamese twin, electromagnetism, has not made our lives better in some respects with its cures and comforts.

---

1 See *Errata* (1997) p. 131 and *Language and Silence* (1967), p. ix.

Who would fault the internet for seeding humanitarian values in places where they don't exist?

Aside from autonomous self-reflection, we have to rely on something more, some basic goodness, to temper the human alloy in its ongoing, suggestive forge into steel-hard coldness. Reinhold Niebuhr, Albert Schweitzer, Simone Weil, the Dalai Lama, Malala Yousafzai, and others of purer heart (and selective denial) have based enviable worldviews on such goodness. As someone who profits from turning people into wash machines and human flies, it's something I'm not worthy enough to sell.

But I'm all for buying.

Bibliography

Books

Abramson, Albert, *The History of Television, 1882-1941* (1987)

Abu Amru Al Qa'idy, *A Course in the Art of Recruiting* (Al-Qaeda manual) (2010)

American Psychiatric Association, *Diagnostic and Statistical Manual of Mental Disorders, Text Revision DSM-5-TR*, American Psychiatric Association (2022)

Arendt, Hannah, *Eichmann in Jerusalem* (1963)

Arons, Harry, *Techniques of Speed Hypnosis* (1953)

Balzac, Honoré de, *The Centenarian* (1822)

Balzac, Honoré de, *Ursule Mirouët* (1841)

Beach, Frank A., *Clark Leonard Hull, a Biographical Memoir* (1959)

Ben-Ghiat, Ruth, *Strongmen, Mussolini to the Present* (2020)

Berman, Sanford I., *A Comparative Treatment of Fact, Inference and Causation in the Theory of Argumentation and of General Semantics* (doctoral thesis) (1958)

Berman, Sanford I., *How to Lessen Misunderstandings* (1962)

Berman, Sanford I., *The Closed Mind* (1965)

Berman, Sanford I., *Why Do We Jump to Conclusions?* (1965)

Berman, Sanford I., *Words, Meaning and People,* (1982)

Berman, Sarah, *Don't Call it a Cult, the Shocking Story of Keith Reniere and the Women of NXIVM* (2021)

Cassirer, Ernst, *The Myth of the State* (1946)

Coleridge, Samuel Taylor, "Ryme of the Ancient Mariner" (1834 version that first appeared in *Lyrical Ballads*, 1798)

Collins, Wilkie, *Woman in White* (1860)

Cook, William Wesley, *Practical Lessons on Hypnotism* (1927)

Coughlin, Con, *Saddam, King of Terror* (2002)

De Laurence, L. W., *Hypnotism, A Complete System of Method, Appreciation and Use* (1900)

Diamond, Peter, *Master Course in Hypnotism* (1972)

Doyle, Arthur Conan, *John Barrington Cowles* (1886)

Doyle, Arthur Conan, *The Parasite* (1894)

du Maurier, George, *Trilby* (1894)

Durkheim, Emile, *The Elementary Forms of the Religious Life* (1954)

Duttlinger, Carolin, *Kafka in Context* (2017)

Eldridge, Edward, *Hypnotism, A Complete System of Method* (1901)

Encyclopedia of Philosophy (1967)

Erelle, Anna, *In the Skin of a Jihadist* (2015)

Fegley, Randall, *Equatorial Guinea, An African Tragedy* (1989)

Feldman, Marc D. Cunnien, Alan J, Hamilton, James C., *Factitious Disorders in Medical and Psychiatric Practices* (2018)

Fisher, Marshall Jon & Fisher, David E., *Tube, the Invention of Television* (1996)

Flint, Dr. Herbert, *Dr. Herbert L. Flint's Hypnotic Routine* (no date, ca. 1897)

Franquin, *Open Your Mind, a Course on Hypnotism* (1954)

Freud, Sigmund, *Jokes and their Relation to the Unconscious* (1905)

Fromm, Erich, *Escape from Freedom* (1949)

Gaskell, Elizabeth, *Cranford* (1851)

Gauld, Alan, *History of Hypnotism* (1992)

Gerdes, Louise I., ed. *Perspectives on Modern World History, the Columbine School Shooting* (2012)

Gleason, Maud W., *Making Men: Sophists and Delf-Presentation in Ancient Rome* (1995)

Guinness Book of World Records (1996)

Haslam, John, *Illustrations of Madness* (1810)

Hassan, Steven, *Combating Cult Mind Control* (2016)

Hawthorne, Nathaniel, *House of the Seven Gables* (1851)

Hawthorne, Nathaniel, *The Blithedale Romance* (1852)

Hull, Clark Leonard, *Hypnosis and Suggestibility*, (1933)

James, Henry, *The Bostonians* (1886)

James, William, *Varieties of Religious Experience* (1917)

Jay, Mike, *A Visionary Madness, the Case of James Tilly Matthews and the Influencing Machine* (2014)

Kimmel, Michael S., *Healing from Hate: How Young Men Get into—and out of—Violent Extremism* (2018)

Korzybski, Count Alfred Habdank, *Science and Sanity* (1933)

Kroger, William, Clinical and Experimental Hypnosis (1977)

Lemov, Rebecca, *World as Laboratory* (2005)

Leonidas, Professor, *Secrets of Stage Hypnotism* (1901)

McGill, Ormond, *Encyclopedia of Stage Hypnotism* (1947)

McGill, Ormond, *Professional Stage Hypnotism* (second edition, 1977)

McGill, Ormond, *Encyclopedia of Stage Hypnotism* (third edition, 1996)

McLean, Donald F., *Restoring Baird's Image* (2000)

Merritt, Rob & Brown, Brooks, *No Easy Answers: The Truth Behind Death at Columbine* (2002)

Michael Cohen, *Disloyal* (2020)

Millar, Fergus, *The Crowd in Rome in the Late Republic* (1998)

Miller, Clarence, *Sparks, Lightning, Cosmic Rays, an Anecdotal History of Electricity*, Dayton (1939)

Morgan, Ted, *Literary Outlaw, the Life and Times of William S. Burroughs* (1988)

Morus, Iwan Rhys, *Frankenstein's Children, Electricity, Exhibition, and Experiment in Early Nineteenth-Century London* (1998)

Mowatt, Anna Cora, *Autobiography of an Actress* (1854)

Orizio, Riccardo, *Talk of the Devil, Encounters with Seven Dictators* (2002)

Orton, J. Louis, *Hypnotism Made Practical* (1943)

Palmer-Jones, *25 Lessons in Hypnotism* (no date, ca 1955?)

Palmer, John-Ivan, *Master of Deception* (2020)

Pearson, Lionel, *The Art of Demosthenes* (1976)

Pera, Marcello, *The Ambiguous Frog, the Galvani-Volta Controversy on Animal Electricity* (English translation, 1992)

Plessner, Helmuth, *Laughing and Crying, a Study of the Limits of Human Behavior* (1970)

Plutarch, *Morales* (100 AD)

Poe, Edgar Allen, *Complete Tales and Poems* (Dorset Press, 1989)

Polizotti, Mark, *Revolution of the Mind, the Life of André Breton* (1995)

Post, Jerrold M., *Leaders and Their Followers in a Dangerous World, the Psychology of Political Behavior* (2004)

Ritchie, Michael, *Please Stand By, a Prehistory of Television* (1994)

Royal Commission, *Report of the Royal Commission to Investigate Animal Magnetism* (1784)

Saslow, Eli, *Rising out of Hatred, the Awakening of a Former White Nationalist* (2018)

Schlathoelter, Rev. Louis F., *Hypnotism Explained* (1898)

Schnackenberg, Gertrude, *Throne of Labdacus* (2000)

Schwartz, Evan I, *The Last Lone Inventor, David Sarnoff vs Philo T. Farnsworth, a tale of Genius, Deceit, and the birth of Television* (2002)

Sextus, Carl, *Hypnotism, a Correct Guide to the Science and How Subjects are Influenced* (ca 1893)

Shoumatoff, Alex, *African Madness* (1988)

Simi, Pete & Futrell, Robert, *American Swastika, Inside the White Power Movement's Hidden Spaces of Hate* (2010)

Simi, Pete and Futrell, Robert, *American Swastika* (2010)

Simon, Linda, *Dark Light* (2004)

Steiner, George, *Errata* (1997)

Steiner, George, *Language and Silence* (1967)

Stern, Alexandra, *Proud Boys and the White Ethnostate* (2019)

Storr, Anthony, *Feet of Clay, Saints, Sinners and Madmen: a Study of Gurus* (1996)

Szymborska, Wisława, *Miracle Farm, Select Poems* (2001)

Theroux, Paul, *Fresh Air Fiend* (2000)
Titze, Dr. Ingo R., *Principles of Voice Production* (1994)
Turner, Lana, *The Lady, The Legend, the Truth* (1982)
van Pelt, S. J., *Hypnotism and the Power Within* (1951)
Vera, Rocco Dal ed., *The Voice in Violence, Essays on Voice and Speech* (2001)

Wexler, Stuart, *America's Secret Jihad, the Hidden History of Religious Terrorism in the United States* (2015)
Wilbur, Richard, *New and Collected Poems* (1989)
Willis, Martin & Wynne, Catherine, *Victorian Literary Mesmerism* (1994)
Winters, Alison, *Mesmerized: Powers of Mind in Victorian Britain* (1998)
Yahia Latif, *I Was Saddam's Son* (1997)
Young, L. E., *25 Lessons in Hypnotism* (no date, ca 1925?)

Periodicals

American Journal of Clinical Hypnosis
Arizona Business Gazette
Arizona Star
Blackwood's Magazine
Canadian Journal of Neurological Sciences
Chicago Magazine
Chicago Today
Chicago Tribune
Chronicle of Education
Daily Beast
Daily Telegraph
Daily Mail
Edinburgh Magazine
Guardian
Ha'aretz Magazine
Irish Sun
Isis
Journal of Deradicalization
London Times
Los Angeles Times
Mail & Guardian
Minneapolis Star-Tribune
New Dawn
New Republic
New York Daily Tribune
New York Post

New York Times
Newsweek
Philadelphia Inquirer
Proceedings of the National Academy of Science
Public Discourse
San Francisco Chronicle
Saturday Evening Post
Sun Newspapers (Minneapolis)
The Diplomat
The Economist
The Police Gazette
Time Magazine
Virginian (Virginia, Minnesota)
Washington Post

Websites

ABCNews.com
ageofempires.com
businessinsider.com
CBSNews.com
CNN.com
(Congressional Research Service) crsreports.congress.gov
ConsumerHealthDigest #04-14 (dead link)
(Council on Foreign Relations) cfr.org
edweek.org
en.wikipedia.org
engramma.it
forums.ageofempires.com
hearinghealthmatters.org
history.com
latimes.com
leevonk.com
Mass-murderFandom.com
meaww.com
Minnesotapublicradio.org
msn.com
nbcnews.com
newgrounds.com
newyorker.com
pagebypagebooks.com
policechiefmagazine.org

QuackWatch.org (dead link)
rationalwiki.org
realclearpolitics.com
robertdavisinc.com
SignOnSanDiego.com
thecircumlocationoffice.com
thehistoryhub.com
the zebra.com
ukessays.com
USAToday.com
usma.edu
vlex.co.uk
webharvest.gov
Wikipedia.org
Youtube.com

Other sources

Department of Justice, U.S. Attorney's Office, District of Arizona
Marshall JCM Handbook (1998)
Manchurian Candidate, directed by John Frankenheimer (1962)
Pima Co. Arizona Case No A-25150, Fische 11, Minute Entry B2 (1974)
Pima Co. Arizona Case No A-25150, Item B16
U.S. Department of Justice Press Release (Los Angeles Office)
Wild Country Netflix Series (2018)

Name Index

Aldini, Giovanni 106
Amichai, Yahuda 30
Amin, Idi 145, 150, 151
Andreas-Salomé, Lou 46
Arendt, Hannah 168
Arklöv, Jackie 123-24
Arons, Harry 41
Baird, John Logie 110-12, 114
Baldwin, George 80
Balzac, Honoré de 80, 95, 101-2
Baron, Edwin 98, 119, 139, 154, 166
Bataille, George 144
Bedloe 97
Ben-Ghiat, Ruth 149n
Benedich, Ivan 98
Berman, Michele 75
Berman, Sandra 75
Berman, Sanford I. (see Dean, Dr. Michael) 62, 71-2, 75
Biden, President 155
Bilel 141
Bill the King 108
Bishop, Elizabeth 38
Bloom, Harold 61
Bogan, Louise 37
Bokassa, Jean-Bédel 147, 149-50
Bolgstrom, Sune 68
Bolsonaro, Jair 148
Boone, Edwin 23
Bose, George Mathias 104
Boyne, Gil 76
Braunn, Dr. Bennett 24
Breton, André 17, 26
Brievek, Anders 124
Brunoni 97
Brutus 94
Burgus, Patricia 24
Burroughs, William 63
Caesar, Julius 94
Carson, Johnny 64
Cassirer, Ernst 118

Casson, Peter 112
Cavendish, Henry 105
Chagnon, Napoleon 167
Chambige, Henri 98
Chateaubriand 97
Chekhov, Anton 108
Cleveland, Grover 89
Cohen, Michael 148
Coleridge, Samuel Taylor 101
Collins, Pat 72, 146
Collins, Wilkie 80
Connolly, Cyril 32
Cook, William 41
Cooper, Anderson 156n
Coughlin, Father Charles 152
Coverdale 101
Cowles, John Barrington 97, 101
Crasilneck, Dr. Harold B. 23-4
Crusius, Patrick 119
Cummings, E. E. 37
Cunnien, Dr. Alan J. 52n, 59
Dalai Lama 169
Dalí, Salvador 147
Dante, Elizabeth 67
Dante, Lee 70
Dante, Ronald 64-76
Dante, Sage 76
Davis Jr., Sammy 64
De Laurence, L. W. 41
Dean, Dr. Michael (see Berman, Sanford I.) 62-73, 75-6, 159
Democles 17
Demosthenes 87-9
Devil 129
Diamond, Peter 41
Dickens, Charles 89
Doolittle, Hilda 37
Doyle, Arthur Conan 80, 97, 101
Dracula 95
Dryden, John 100
Durkheim, Emile 160-1

Eichmann, Adolf 168
Eldridge, Edward 41
Elizabeth, Queen 157
Elvis 65, 94
Erelle, Anna 141
Eubuludes of Miletus 162
Faria, Abbé José-Custodio de 80, 97
Farnsworth, Philo 105n, 111-12, 114
Farnsworth, Professor Frank 22, 118
Flint, Dr. Herbert 40, 100
Foissac, Dr. 95
Fos, José Antonio García-Trevijano 145
Fosco, Count 80
Foster, George 106
Frankenstein 106, 109
Franklin, Benjamin 9n, 103-5, 137
Franquin 41
Freud, Sigmund 45-6, 113
Fromm, Erich 118
Futrell, Robert 124
Gaddafi, Muammar 148
Galvani, Luigi 104-6
Garland, Judy 83
Gaskell, Elizabeth 97
Gates, Christopher 23-4
Gatewood, Philip 71-3, 75
Gerstenberger, Dr. Dean 24
GhostEzra 155
Ginsberg, Alan 37
Gonzales, Dr. Castillo 149-50
Gaede Sisters 121
Gray, Anderson 99
Great Maurice 41-4, 46, 61, 126, 141, 149
Grille, Madeleine 98
Gurdjieff, Georgei 159
Gutierrez, Jose 78, 80-2
Hackett, Buddy 64
Hall, Dr. James A. 23
Hannusen, Erik Jan 101-2
Harper, Margaret 19
Harris, Eric 136-7
Hassan, Steven 160n, 161

Hawthorne, Nathaniel 96, 100-01
Hayakawa, S. J. 62
Hayward, Harry 99
Heap, Dr. Michael 25
Heidegger, Martin 168
Heron of Alexandria 153
Hilgard, Ernest 44
Hills, Holly 50
Hitler, Adolf 11, 74, 101-2, 113, 125, 135, 137-8, 146-8, 152, 157
Holgrave 80
Hope, Bob 34, 36, 64
Horace 100
Howarth, Lynn 19
Hull, Clark Leonard 112-14
Hussein, Saddam 146, 149, 151
Hussein, Uday 149
Husserl, Edmund 123, 167
James, Henry 96
James, William 44, 160
Jeffers, Lawrence 66
Jezebel 46
Johnson, Louise N. 48
Jones, Jim 160
Joplin, Janis 83
Kafka, Franz 143
Kahlo, Frida 54
Kant, Immanuel 44, 123
Kensington, Bob 70
Khomeini, Ayatollah 141
Kim Il Sung 145
Kimmel, Michael 121
King Kleagle 118
King, Angela 122
Klebold, Dylan 136-7
Kleinhauz, Dr. Morris 19
Kolisch, John 80
Korzybski, Count Alfred Habdank 62-3, 71-2, 75
Kroger, Dr. William 23
Lafontaine, Charles 80
Lanterman, Mark 142
Lanza, Adam 134

Leitner, Konradi 40
Leonidas, Professor 41
Leopold, Mark 156
Lincoln, Abraham 89
Linkletter, Art 114
Louis XVI, King 9, 103, 105, 114, 121, 124, 136, 138, 143, 155
Lowell, Robert 37, 61
Lucas, George 57
MacHovec, Dr. Frank 19, 23-4
Manson, Charles 101, 123
Mariam, Mengistu Haile 150
Marianine 95, 101
Marx, Harpo 65
Masserman, Dr. Jules 24
Matthews, Tilly 107-8
Maule, Thomas 96, 101
Maurier, George du 96
McCouts, William F. 142
McDonald, Thomas 99
McGill, Ormond 40, 76, 113, 140
McKenna, Paul 23
McVeigh, Timothy 124
Meeks, Gregory 156
Merton, Thomas 162
Mesmer, Anton 9, 14, 19, 63, 80, 94, 103, 103-10, 115, 124, 136-7, 143, 148, 154
Meyers, Dr. Russell 63
Milošević?, Mirjana 150
Milošević?, Slobodan 150, 151
Minow, Newton 114
Mirouët, Ursule 102
Moore, Marianne 37-8
Morgan, Ted 63
Moseley, Maj. Gen. George Van Horn 152
Mowatt, Anna Cora 166
Murdoch, Rupert 107
Murrow, Edward R. 114
Mussolini 149, 168
Nabokov, Vladimir 54
Napoleon 147, 167
Neukor 98

Nguema, Francisco Macías 145-6, 149
Niebuhr, Reinhold 169
Nipkow, Paul 108
Northcott, Miss Kate 101
Obote, Milton 145
Ogden, Emily 147
Orton, J. Louis 138
Palmer-Jones 41
Patton (hypnotic victim) 99
Peller, Ronald (see Ronald Dante) 75
Penclosa, Madame Helen 80, 97, 101
Perskyi, Constantin 108
Peter (Dr. Dante's victim) 73-4
Picciolini, Christian 121-3
Plath, Sylvia 37-8
Plessner, Helmuth 10, 43
Plutarch 87, 91
Poe, Edgar Allan 96
Post, Jerrold 140
Pound, Ezra 168
Prince, Morton 44
Putin, Vladimir 148
Pyncheon, Gervayse 96
Q 152-6
Quincey, Thomas de 95
Rae, Shelly 50
Rajneesh, Bhagwan 160
Ramos, Humberto 81-7
Randi, James 26, 141
Raz, Dr. Amir 163-5
Realmuto, Dr. George 134
Robertz, Frank 138
Rockwell, Norman 152
Roof, Dylan 119-20, 122
Rose, David 43
Rosing, Boris 108
S. M. (hypnotic victim) 94
Saint-Aubin, Dr. 96
Salzman, Nancy 159
Sanders, Tywanza 120
Santanelli 21
Sarnoff, David 112
Schlathoelter, Louis 41

Schnackenberg, Gertrude 105
Schopenhauer, Arthur 15
Schweitzer, Albert 169
Self, Will 21
Sennevoy, Jules du Potet de 80
Sextus, Carl 41
Shakespeare, William 89, 138
Sharpe, Jennifer 64
Shelley, Mary 106
Shook, Brian 70, 73-4
Shorter, Dr. Edward 134
Simi, Pete 124
Skinner, B.F. 15, 164
Sobel, Dave 50
Socrates 166
Soleimani, Gen. Qasem 157
Spearman, Dianna 147
Stalin, Joseph 168
Steinbart, Austin Ryan 153
Steiner, George 168
Steinhäuser, Robert 138
Stern, Alexandra 119
Stevens, Wallace 37
Stokes, Terry 116
Stookie Bill 110
Storr, Anthony 162
Svengali 80, 96-7, 99-101, 119, 141
Swayze, John Cameron 110
Swift, Rev. Wesley Arthur 118
Tabarn, Sharon 20n
Taggard, Genevieve 38
Tapley, William 156
Tarrant, Brenton 120
Tarrant, Dr. 96
Tate, Allen 61
Taubman, Judge Alice 67
Templeton, Dr. 97
Theroux, Paul 27, 167n
Tinkerbell 44
Titze, Dr. Ingo R. 88
Townsend, Dr. 22
Tranz, Justin 148
Trilby 96-7, 99

Trump, Donald 119, 147-8, 152, 155n
Tullius 95
Turner, Lana 61, 64-5, 67, 69-70
Valdemar, M. 96
Van Pelt, Dr. S.J. 41
Vandermeide, Ben 80, 151
Vespasian, Emperor 18
Vixen, Veronica 30, 37
Volta, Alesandro 104, 107
Wagner, Ed 69
Walsh, David 134
Warner, Sylvia Townsend 37
Weil, Simone 169
Weise, Jeff 133-8
Welch, Edgar Maddison 155
Welles, Orson 109, 115
Wellington, Duke of 104
Westervelt, Professor 100
Wiegand, Steven 124
Wilbur, Richard 18, 38
Wilde, Oscar 89
Wilson, Kenneth G. 68
Winrod, Rev. Gerald 152
Wis?awa Szymborska 117
Wittgenstein, Ludwig 123
Wood, Lin 155
Young, L. E. 40
Yousafzai, Malala 169
Zimmerman, Mrs. (hypnotic victim) 95
Zworykin, Vladimir 108, 114

www.ingramcontent.com/pod-product-compliance
Lightning Source LLC
Chambersburg PA
CBHW062056270326
41931CB00013B/3098